Crossing Enemy Lines One Nation Under God

Tina M. Ray

Bloomington, IN Milton Keynes, UK

authorHOUSE®

AuthorHouse™
1663 Liberty Drive, Suite 200
Bloomington, IN 47403
www.authorhouse.com
Phone: 1-800-839-8640

AuthorHouse™ UK Ltd.
500 Avebury Boulevard
Central Milton Keynes, MK9 2BE
www.authorhouse.co.uk
Phone: 08001974150

First published by AuthorHouse 5/4/2007

ISBN: 978-1-4343-0597-8 (sc)

*Printed in the United States of America
Bloomington, Indiana*

This book is printed on acid-free paper.

Contents

Dedications

This book is dedicated to my Lord and savior Jesus Christ, who willingly gave His life so we would have eternal life through the death, burial, and resurrection.

He came to seek and save that which was lost, He shed innocent blood for the remission of our sins. He was the sinless, blameless lamb of Calvary.

He was slain for our transgressions, bruised for our iniquities, He bore our sorrows and by His stripes we are healed. He lives in each and every believer's heart; He is the eternal hope of glory. He came to do His father's will. He raised the dead, healed the wounded and afflicted, opened blinded eyes, walked on water, changed water into wine, smote the rock to bring forth water in the desert, parted the red sea. There are so many things Jesus did I could write a book on Him alone. The promises in His word are too many to mention. He never leaves us or forsakes us, He extends mercy and grace. He carries our burdens. He carries us through our trials, sheltering us beneath His wings. Imagine our creator who has the earth as His foot stool. How powerful, majestic and almighty! There have been thousands of songs sung unto Him. He inhabits the praises of His people. Lift up your voice and sing praises unto Him. Praise your name Jesus! Praising you forever.

Psalm 147:5 Great is our Lord, and of great power: His understanding is infinite.

Acknowledgements

I have written two books of poetry, both books have been a blessing in my life.

The second book however, exceeded my expectations, and I give my Lord and savior, Jesus the full credit for the inspirational creativity He has placed within. I would like to extend thanks to my right hand man Ryan McConnell, who has been there every step of the way, from signing the agreement, to the book orders to the promotions. Thanks Ryan. I would also like to mention how dedicated the design team is in creating exactly what you want when you choose your cover.

You guys are great. I would like to personally thank my pastor, Windell Pell for teaching the deep words and spiritual truths of God's word. Thank you from the bottom of my heart. I would like to acknowledge special friends who are first prayer warriors, and secondly good listeners as they help to critique my work.

Thank you Kim, Connie, Moni, and my best friend Gina. May God bless you all and shine His face upon your lives. I would like to tell you that as a first time novelist I knew there would be challenges in this type of writing, but it made me more eager to bring you the truth. There are endless hours of research at your local libraries and internet surfing, and hitting those old history books I hadn't looked at in years. I pray as you read my novel that you will have a clearer understanding of how valuable our prayer life should be and we live in a free country, others aren't so blessed to know freedom. America the beautiful get back to the days of old and bring old glory to Jesus, let's hold up the blood stained banner for the cause of the freedom to worship One Nation under God.

Psalm 148:1-2 Praise ye the Lord. Praise ye the Lord from the heavens: praise Him in the heights.

Praise ye Him, all His angels: praise ye Him, all His hosts.

In God We Trust

Let us take a journey, a trip down memory lane, let us go back to history where the archives of freedom began. It is a bright sunny June day and we are traveling to Philadelphia, the city of brotherly love. We arrive to see a round table discussion, hands clasped in prayer, heads bowed in reverence as if someone were there. They are united in prayer to God giving honor unto Him. This is how they start their day before they can begin. Richard Henry Lee brings to the table a resolution urging Congress to declare freedom. After much discussion they come to a resolution to vote it in. On June 11th there is an appointed committee to draft a declaration of independence, on that committee was Benjamin Franklin, Thomas Jefferson, John Adams, Robert Livingston and Roger Sherman. Jefferson drafts a rough copy and the committee reviews it, it is a fair copy. On the first of July through the fourth congress revises and debates The Declaration of Independence. Signed into Congress on July 4th-1776 are the names of the fifty six signatures who signed The Declaration of Independence.

From Pennsylvania: James Wilson, George Ross, Benjamin Franklin, John Morton, George Taylor, Robert Morris, Benjamin Rush, James Smith, and George Clymer.

From Massachusetts: Samuel Adams, John Hancock, Robert Treat Paine, John Adams, and Elbridge Gerry. From Delaware: Caesar Rodney,

Thomas McKean and George Read. From New Jersey: John Hart, Abraham Clark, Richard Stockton, and Francis Hopkinson. From Georgia: Lyman Hall, George Walton, and Button Gwinnett. From North Carolina: John Penn, William Hooper, and Joseph Hewes. From South Carolina: Thomas Heyward, jr. Edward Rutledge, Arthur Middleton, and Thomas Lynch, jr. From New York: William Floyd, Francis Lewis, Philip Livingston and Lewis Morris. From Rhode Island: William Ellery, and Stephen Hopkins. From Virginia: Thomas Jefferson, Francis Lightfoot Lee, Thomas Nelson, jr. Richard Henry Lee, Carter Braxton, George Wythe, and Benjamin Harrison. From New Hampshire: William Whipple, Josiah Bartlett, and Mathew Thornton. From Maryland: William Paca, Thomas Stone, Samuel Chase and Charles Carroll. From Connecticut: Roger Sherman, William Williams, Oliver Wolcott, and Samuel Huntington. Each of these signers plays an important role in shaping our history. The Declaration of Independence instituted the want, will and hopes of the people. All men are created equal, and they are endowed by their Creator with certain unalienable rights, among which is life, liberty, and pursuit of happiness. It is the right of the people to alter or abolish it, and to institute new government, laying it's foundation on such principles. The

Enforcement of those constitutional provisions intended to secure that equality of rights which is the foundation of free government. This famous document reflects the turmoil and excitement of the birth of a nation. The spiritual cornerstone of The United States is at the heart of America's continuous quest to live up to it's founding ideas. America's Founding Fathers: John Blair of Virginia was born in 1732 at Williamsburg. He studied law at London's Middle Temple. In 1776 he took part in the Virginia Constitutional Convention, he sat on the committee which framed the declaration of rights and as well the plan for a new government. Blair was named by Washington in 1789 as an associate justice of the U.S. Supreme Court where he helped decide many cases (important cases). In 1796 he resigned that position and spent his last remaining years in Williamsburg. He was sixty eight years of age when he died. James Madison of Virginia was born in 1751 the oldest of ten children. He served on the Orange County committee for safety, he also advocated for various revolutionary steps which framed the Virginia Constitution in the House of Delegates (1776-77). In The Council of State in 1778-80 he also served. Due to his ill health he could not serve military status. He dominated the framing of the Constitution by guiding the Constitution through the Continental Congress. He kept journals of the republican principles which helped the laws to be established through the government. In 1789-97 in the U.S. House of Representatives he helped to ensure the passage of The Bill of Rights. In 1809-17 James Madison was our fourth president. He died on June 28-1836. George Mason of Virginia was born in 1725. When George was ten years of age his father died and he was in the care of his uncle's upbringing. He was very established and was one of the richest planters in Virginia. He later pursued his political interests. He became justice of The Fairfax County court. He was elected to The Virginia House of Burgess in 1759. He framed the first part of The Declaration of Independence which was a model for Jefferson widely copied in other colonies and was the basis for the Federal constitution Bill of Rights. Throughout his career Mason was known as and has been called the American Manifestation of the Enlightenment. On October 7-1792 Mason died. James Mc Clurg of Virginia was born in 1746. He graduated the College of William and Mary in 1762. At the University of Edinburgh he received his degree in postgraduate medical studies. He was known as one of the most eminent physicians in Virginia. Mc Clurg also pursued politics and served on Virginia's executive council. He died on July 9-1823. Edmund Randolph of Virginia was born on August 10-1753. He attended the college of William and Mary and continued his education by studying the law. He was the youngest member of the convention at age 23, and served as an aide-de-camp to General Washington. He also attended the convention that adopted Virginia's first state constitution in 1776. Randolph become governor of Virginia in 1786 and was a delegate to the Annapolis Convention. He helped create a strong central government comprised of three branches, legislative, executive and judicial. He enabled the legislative to veto state laws and use force against states which failed to fulfill their duties. He died at the age of sixty in 1813. George Washington of Mount Vernon Virginia was the eldest of six children. In 1753 Washington began his military career. He became appointed as a major in the militia by the royal governor. In 1754-63 was the French and Indian war which Washington led troops into challenge French control of the Ohio River, but met defeat at Fort Necessity, Pa. Congress appointed him as commander and chief after the blood shed at Lexington and Concord in 1775. Washington was the first president of the United States in 1789-97. He died December 14-1799 in Mount Vernon. George Wythe of Virginia was born in 1726. He was the middle child. He received very little education but was to become a jurist and teacher. Later he was sent to Prince George County to read law. At the age of twenty he became associated with a lawyer in Spotsylvania County. From the mid 1750s-1775 he served on The House of Burgess. In 1779 the chair of law in a U. S. institution of higher learning was created and Jefferson and other officials appointed Wythe to fill that position. James Monroe, John Marshall amongst some of the earliest college trained lawyers Wythe educated while in that position. Wythe died at the age of eighty in 1806 in Richmond. I chose to write about the Founding Fathers of Virginia because that is where our first president was from. The other Founding Fathers will be recognized by their state. Connecticut: Oliver Ellsworth, William Samuel Johnson, and Roger Sherman. Delaware: George Read, Gunning Bedford Jr. John Dickinson, Richard Bassett and Jacob Broom. Georgia: William Few,

Abraham Baldwin, William Houston, William L. Pierce. Maryland: James Mc Henry, Daniel of St. Thomas Jenifer, Daniel Carroll, Luther Martin, and John F. Mercer. Massachusetts: Nathaniel Gorham, Rufus King, Elbridge Gerry, and Caleb Strong. New Hampshire: John Langdon, and Nicholas Gilman. New Jersey: William Livingston, David Brearly (Brearley), William Paterson (Patterson) Jonathan Dayton, and William Houston. New York: Alexander Hamilton, John Lansing Jr., and

Robert Yates. North Carolina: William Blount, Richard Dobbs Spaight, Hugh Williamson, William R. Davie, and Alexander Martin. Pennsylvania: Benjamin Franklin, Thomas Mifflin, Robert Morris, George Clymer, Thomas Fitzsimons (Fitzsimons), James Ingersoll, James Wilson, and Gouverneur Morris. Rhode Island did not send any delegates to the Constitutional Convention. South Carolina: John Rutledge, Charles Cotesworth, Pinckney, Charles Pinckney, and Pierce Butler. The Chronology (order) of Events that helped shape our nation 1776-77 is: 1776: June 7- Congress, meeting in Philadelphia, Richard Henry Lee's resolution urging Congress to declare independence. June 11- Benjamin Franklin, Robert Livingston, John Adams, Thomas Jefferson, were appointed to a committee to draft a declaration of independence. June 12-27 at the request of the committee Jefferson drafts a declaration; the "original rough draft" is reviewed and is a "fair copy". June 28- Jefferson's "fair copy "is read. by the committee. July 1-4 The Declaration of Independence is debated and revised by Congress. July 2- Congress declares independence as the army and British fleet arrive in New York. July 4- In the morning of a bright sunny cool day, in Philadelphia Congress adopts the Declaration of Independence. John Dunlap prints the Declaration of Independence. They are now called "Dunlap Broadsides." There are twenty four copies known to exist. Two are in the Library of Congress. One of these was Washington's personal copy. July 5- John Hancock, president of the Continental Congress, dispatches the first of Dunlap Broadsides of the Declaration of Independence to the legislatures of Delaware and New Jersey. July 6- The first newspaper rendition of the Declaration of Independence is printed by Pennsylvania Evening Post. July 8- The first pubic reading of the Declaration is in Philadelphia. July 9- Washington orders that the Declaration of Independence be read before the army in New York. July 19- Congress orders the Declaration of Independence officially signed by members. August 2- British reinforcement arrives in New York after being repelled at Charleston S. C. Delegates begins to sign engrossed copy of the Declaration of Independence. 1777- January 18- Congress now sitting in Baltimore Maryland, orders that signed copies of the Declaration be printed by Mary Katherine Goddard of Baltimore. When in the course of human events we hold these truths, the want, and wills and hopes of our people. The history of our motto on our currency is In God We Trust was established largely because of the increased religious sentiment existing during the Civil War. Samuel P. Chase Secretary of the Treasury received many appeals from devout persons through out the country, urging that the United States recognize the Deity on United States coins. One such letter dated November 13-1861 appealed for the recognition of Almighty God in some form on our coins. He wrote" What if our Republic was not shattered beyond reconstruction?" "Would not the antiquaries of succeeding centuries rightly reason from our past that we were a heathen nation?" "What I propose is that instead of the goddess of liberty we shall have next inside the 13 stars a ring inscribed with the words PERPETUAL UNION; within the ring the all seeing eye, crowned with a halo; beneath this eye the American flag, bearing in its field stars equal to the number of the states united; in the folds of the bars the words GOD, LIBERTY. LAW. January 18th-1837 it was found that the Act of Congress prescribed the mottoes and devices that should be placed upon the coins of the United States. This meant that the mint could make no changes without the enactment of additional legislation by the Congress. In December 1863, the Director of the Mint submitted designs for new one-cent, two-cent, and three-cent coin to Secretary Chase for approval. He proposed that upon the designs OUR GOD, OUR COUNTRY or GOD OUR TRUST should appear as a motto on the coins. Chase approved IN GOD WE TRUST. April 22-1864 Congress passed the act. IN GOD WE TRUST is the national motto of the United States. The first paper currency bearing the motto entered circulation on October 1-1957. The mission of the Department of the Treasury is to promote the conditions of prosperity and stability in the United States and encourage prosperity and stability in the rest of the world. The Department of the Treasury is also responsible in a wide range of activities including advising the President on economic and financial promoting the President's growth agenda, and enhancing corporate governance in institutions. There are two major components of the offices and the operating bureaus which carry out the specific operations assigned to the department. They are to include: Producing postage stamps, currency and coinage; supervising national banks and thrift institutions; enforcing federal finance and tax laws; managing federal finances; collecting taxes, duties and monies paid to and due to the U.S. and paying the U. S. managing government accounts and public debt; advising on domestic and international financial; monetary, economic, trade policy; and investigating and prosecuting tax evaders, counterfeiters, and forgers.

Psalm 125:1 They that trust in the Lord shall be as mount Zion, which cannot be removed, but abideth forever.

America The Beautiful!

From your majestic mountains and deepest of blue seas you can be seen.

From the tallest trees to the overlying beauty that you possess painted by the master's hand, ever so intricate and beautiful, stands for his awesome creation.

Look at oceans and streams, the waterfalls, the breath of life in each one of us.

How the stars are set in the sky in their pattern, the solar system, the rotation of the sun, the speed of light. How can anyone deny His power and might? America you became the land of the free and the home of the brave through men and women who trusted in the unseen hand and moved with fear to bring us truth and knowledge and understanding through prayer, the building blocks of the sands of time that connects us with our Lord and Savior Jesus Christ. Jesus gave man knowledge and the truth in His word to establish laws and constitutions which are the framework of the mighty nation we have become. The United States of America. America you once held the standards for a strong nation bathed in prayer and upholding the biblical principles that has made a great nation. Our founding fathers paved the way to truth and life and liberty, but our nation has become tainted by the blackness of sin in our world. So many changes have happened to darken the bluest of skies and majestic mountains, the beauty that is God given. People, without a vision we will perish. A nation that forgets God will fall. If we don't stand for truth, we will fall for anything. Please wake up and honor our motto "In God We Trust." Let us return to the truth and honor and reverence our creator. Give Him glory, and praise, lift up His mighty banner of love, and let us rescue the perishing. One day we will give an account for the truths that were broken and bow on bended knee to the King of Kings and Lord of Lords. I pray for freedom of religion and prayer brought back to our nation.

Psalm 128:1 Blessed is everyone that feareth the Lord; that walketh in His ways.

Prayer Out Of Our School Systems Oh! No

The years roll on, as time marches on. And the unthinkable becomes reality.

The banning of religious practices becomes the target for an atheist leader in 1959 the infamous Madalyn Murray O'Hair entered her son in school in Baltimore only to find out he would be forced to participate in reverential bible reading and unison prayers. An atheist child could only sit in the hallway while his peers prayed. Madalyn did not believe that prayer should be allowed in the school system. Madalyn would brag about spending the day in x-rated movie theaters in down town Baltimore, she was proud that she was the only woman in the theatre watching this filth. Madalyn's life circulated around the filth of the evil in the world. She enjoyed hiring unrepentant criminals to work in her atheist office. She liked the power of employing men who had taken human life. She had a love of power of people. My mother had complete power and control over my brother Jon. Jon was a total slave who was his mother's provider and rescuer. He wasn't allowed to speak to me. He went every where my mother went. They had breakfast, lunch, and dinner everyday together; he went on vacation with her. He never even had the opportunity to date or have a serious relationship with a woman because of the control our mother possessed over him. For twenty years I could not talk to Jon, he would hang up, and tear up letters I sent to him. I was a "Traitor" because I had accepted Christ who had changed my life. My daughter Robin also lived with my mother and was under her evil influence. My mother would have foods high in sugar and fats and called this "living high on the hog."

There was also a cabinet full of booze. My mother also stole huge amounts of money, cheated children out of their inheritances, cheated on taxes, and stole from two of her own companies. She believed "do what thou wilt shall be the only law." Robin was so heavy from the foods she ate, she was unattractive to men, and was controlled by food. My mother began the legal proceedings which would culminate in the United States Supreme Court decision on school prayer with Murray vs. Curlett. There were other cases about school prayer during this time.

One such case was in Pennsylvania, Abingdon Township v. Schemp. Together the two cases were decided and the decision was named. Then on June 16th-1963, the Supreme Court of the United States kicked prayer recitation and Bible reading out of the nation's public schools. The American Atheist celebrated that decision, which upheld our First Amendment right to freedom from religious ceremonies of the Supreme Court's decision. The rule as amended was in violation of the petitioners' rights "to freedom of religion under the First and Fourteenth Amendments" and in violation of "the principle of separation between church and state. (the petitioner in this case was Madalyn Murray O' Hair) To recap our Religion, History, and Government, "The history of man is inseparable from the history of religion. Since the beginning of that history many people devoutly believed that More things are wrought by prayer than this world dreams of. The facts that were written about Madalyn Murray O'Hair were referenced by her son William, who witnessed the horror of demonic influence in his mother's character, watched her gain power with the dark side. The last ten years of Madalyn's life she became more vulgar and profane as the demons she courted got their final hold on her. Madalyn, Jon and Robin were kidnapped and were held for almost thirty days, while Jon tried to raise ransom money for their lives.

Jon wanted to be his mother's rescuer and provider, but died for his faithfulness.

In January 2000, in Camp Wood, Texas, the dismembered bodies of Madalyn, Jon and Robin were found. One of the killers, David Walters led authorities to the site in return for a lighter sentence of serving his time in a federal prison, rather than Texas state prison. He died in prison of liver disease in 2003. A second killer was sentenced a life term in prison. "The fool hath said in his heart, there is no God." Psalms 14:1. William Murray O 'Hair has written a book entitled, "My Life Without God." To bring to light the darkness of his mother's murders, the convicted, the facts surrounding Madalyn's life and his personal conviction of finding Christ in the midst of controversy. The battles he endured while fighting the good fight of faith for the cause of Christ. Yearning for his family to find the same treasure of eternal life he had found, the untold riches of the after life that leads us to our creator, Jesus Christ. William prayed for his mother, brother and daughter to find the love of Christ, while he testified of God's love, lived the life of a Christian soldier, and set an example of servitude to unbelievers. There are still ramifications of having taken prayer out of our school systems which still ring true today. In the last decade we watched in horror as children in our school systems took guns to school and committed the unthinkable crimes of school massacre. There were other copy cat shootings each with the real results of people carried out in body bags. Children bucking authority of school officials, teachers and friends or someone who "hurt their feelings." What are we teaching our kids? We need to be teaching them biblical principles of forgiveness, being tender hearted, as Christ hath forgiven us. There have been children as young as eight, who have been put into juvenile authority for carrying a weapon, carrying out threats of violence etc. What about an accidental shooting? I say the children need better, safer parental observation at all times. Discipline has fallen by the wayside because children are allowed to get away with more than they once were. I blame the media and the school systems for brainwashing our children to go against what is right, when most of the time it is a "right discipline" and a proper action for unruly behavior. Why is there such a need for programs for troubled children? Because someone doesn't want the responsibility of a child or children who will not bend to the rules, no matter what a parent does. So do I think our children need to be raised by a village? No. With all the influence our media and schools have on our children, it is no wonder we have lost control of raising non-violent, respectful children in our world today. I have known many families who have home schooled their children and I have seen a very good change in these children, who have the one on one attention to their educational needs as well as spiritual needs being met. These kids are not missing out on much; they can have socialization of friends, as well as field trips, and the safety of their own homes. To point out safety, how about on a typical October morning, a one-room Amish community school is in session and in comes Charles Carl Roberts, with ammunition, guns, and a heart of violence. He has the boys in this school go outside and lets some of the teachers and teacher's aides go outside, he takes the lives of five Amish girls and injures five others, he then takes his own life. The police try to talk to him, prior to his rage upon the innocent. His wife at a nearby church has met for morning prayer. Here the Amish community has a tragedy, and no rhyme or reason for this to happen. With forgiving hearts, the Amish forgive him and bury their own. It is a day of quiet solitude as the Amish buggies follow each other through the streets to the cemetery to lie to rest their children. What a random act of senseless violence. The Amish community does not have ill feelings or hatred for Charles' wife and children, only forgiveness and mercy and sympathy for her loss as well. Their religion has taught them to forgive others, and they dutifully have done this. With Gods help, I pray they will heal and see their children again one day when Jesus returns with His saints. It is wonderful to see the community's involvement with an outpouring of love, and generosity, through fund raising efforts and cash donations to the Amish. Radio stations have advertised and set up information to help in these efforts. No one really knows or understands why Charles would lash out at the Amish, he to was home schooled as a child. God can forgive the vilest of sinners. I pray everyone learns to have forgiveness in their hearts, and acknowledges our creator Christ Jesus and follows His servitude as He has set an example unto us, His followers.

Continue to pray for our brethren, widow of Charles, and their three children. Since this has happened there has been three or more other school violent acts across our nation. Our school children should never fear safety when they enter the classroom. However, upon taking all necessary precautions of lock down, search anyone and everyone who comes into the school system, this is what our children have to look forward to, to remain safe in our schools. What are next the airport terminals in our hallways? Has our world became so brutal that no one is safe anywhere? If this world continues on a downward spiral of evil, we will have to take extra measures of protecting our loved ones. My prayer for America is that she will bow on bended knee, in total submission of allowing God to bring prayer back to our nation's classrooms, court rooms, etc. to begin to heal and soothe our nation as we get back to the days of old. We will uphold biblical principles, observe the Ten Commandments in our legislative and judicial systems, and stay One Nation Under God. By surrendering unto our Lord and Savior, Jesus Christ, we can embrace what He wants in our nation. We can have the peace that passes all understanding, the joy that is given through the act of obedience, trusting Jesus to protect our nation. We are in the days, when in fact we will have to fight for the rights of religious freedom. There are people who would like to see In God We Trust taken off of our currency, the Ten Commandments taken out of our court systems so that we will have no biblical standards to live by. We cannot allow them to take this from us. These are the standards our forefathers brought to us in the earlier archives of history, and trusted and believed in. Quotes from our sixteenth president, Abraham Lincoln are: "Fellow citizens, we cannot escape history." "Let us have faith that right makes right; and in that faith let us to the end, dare to do our duty as we understand it." "Character is like a tree and reputation its shadow, the shadow is what we think of it; the tree is the real thing." "I can see how it might be possible for a man to look down upon the earth and be an atheist, but I cannot conceive how he could look up unto the heavens and say there is no God. Psalm 1:1 Blessed is the man that walketh not in the counsel of the ungodly, nor standeth in the way of sinners, nor sitteth in the seat of the scornful.

"I Declare War"

The President's Call

The media overtakes our television sets as Iraq totally rejects what the U.S.

Sanctions are and the warnings given for ridding Iraq's weapons of mass destruction. Saddam Hussein was given time to leave Iraq. He completely rejected President Bush's warnings. On March 19-2003, Fighter Squadron led air strikes, and began conducting military operations, against Iraq designed to disarm Iraq of its weapons of mass destruction and to remove the Iraqi Regime from power. Less than two hours after the deadline expired for Saddam, the sound of air raid sirens were heard in Baghdad. President Bush then addresses the nation. "We have enemies, who wish to do harm." "I declare war." The sound rings out throughout our nation, we are now at war. Coalition forces were already in the early" stages of military operations to disarm Iraq, to free its people and to defend the world from grave danger. Operation Iraqi Freedom consisted of the largest special operations force since the Vietnam War. Special forces were also responsible for attacking a number of specific targets such as: weapons of mass destruction sites, airfields, and to command and control headquarters. The military objectives for Operation Iraqi Freedom were to end the regime of Saddam Hussein, identify, isolate and eliminate Iraq's weapons of mass destruction, to search for, capture, and drive out terrorists from the country. Collect intelligence related to terrorist networks, global network of illicit weapons of mass destruction, to end sanctions and to immediately deliver humanitarian support to the many needed citizens and the displaced, to secure Iraq's oil fields, and resources, which belong to the Iraqi people, and to help Iraq create conditions for a transition to a representative self-government. The faces of the fallen are the scenes we envision in our mind's eye, in a war torn country. The first three weeks of war are what I would like to share with you. On March 20-2003, forty missiles and strikes led by 2 F-117s from the 8th fighter squadron arrive. March 21st, Two U.S. marines died in combat. The first marine died after leading his infantry platoon in a fire fight to secure an oil pumping station in southern Iraq. The second while taking actions against Iraqi enemy forces. March 22, the 1-15th Infantry Regiment assaulted the airfield inflicting serious losses on Iraq's 11th infantry division, which was defending the location. March 23rd Iraqi began a new strategy of luring U.S. troops by intending to surrender, only to open fire on the U.S. marines as they came closer. March 24th it was reported that a PATRIOT firing battery "successfully intercepted and destroyed "an incoming Iraqi tactical ballistic missile during an attack on the U.S. and coalition forces in Kuwait. All raids against the Iraqi capital, Baghdad, and the northern city of Mosul continue. March 25th over central Iraq, powerful sandstorms blackened the skies slowing coalition forces. (Limiting visibility). March 26th In the Persian Gulf, naval forces also had to limit flight operations due to limited visibility. March 27th with improved weather coalition air operations increased, a B-2 bomber struck a communications facility in Baghdad. March 28th in southern Iraq, coalition forces captured the Basra oil refinery. March 29th the Iraqi regime warned that suicide attacks would be used against U.S. forces. March 30th Iraqi army and paramilitary units threatens U.S. troops moving north. March 31st the longest night of flights and sorties since the war began. The ground war moved closer to Baghdad, pilots flew nearly fifty sorties. April 1st there are no indications that Iraqi forces are ready to surrender. April 2nd in central Iraq at 7:30 pm

A U-H-60 Black Hawk helicopter crashed. April 3rd relief supplies begin arriving in UM Qasr (a port at Iraq's southern most tip. April 4th the 1st Brigade Combat Team, 3rd Infantry Division (mechanized) completed the capture of Saddam International Airport. April 5th Overnight, coalition aircraft struck the residence of

Saddam Hussein's cousin, Ali Hassan Al-Majid. April 6th the British forces had recovered the remains of Ali Hassan Al- Majid (the senior Iraqi officer in southern Iraq. April 7th following a two week siege, in southern Iraq, British forces took control of Basra. April 8th marine forces captured the headquarters of the Iraqi 10th Division. April 9th the third week into this war, the world watched as U. S. soldiers tore down a statue of Saddam Hussein in front of a large, enthusiastic crowd of Iraqi citizens. The Iraqi citizens are taking all the spoil Saddam has taken from them over the years; there is looting in the streets of Baghdad as the bronze statue of their feared leader comes toppling down. This is symbolic crumbling of Iraqi leader Saddam Hussein's regime going to ruins before their very eyes. Iraqi's people cheered and waved as the military were welcomed on their streets. While the chaos of the war still remains, their feared leader has now gone into hiding. There are portraits of the dictator are being drug through the streets. A brief biography of Saddam was, he was born a peasant on April 28th, 1937, north of Baghdad in a rural town of Tikrit, born into a very poor family. After moving to Baghdad as a teenager, Saddam joined the Arab Baath Socialist Party and initially dedicated to socialism, pan- Arab, and secularism. Over a period of ten – twelve years Saddam accumulated power. In 1979 Saddam took over as president as Al- Bakr stepped down. On buildings and monuments throughout the country his image was everywhere. People couldn't escape Saddam's gaze. Crowds cheered as he took his place as their leader. Thousands voiced support for his policies. Most people would fear for their lives if they went in opposition against him. Saddam had a secret police which would protect him. He was politically savvy, supremely powerful and maliciously brutal. Saddam was obsessed with security, image, and hygiene; he would forbid any journalist from videoing him walking any distance. Saddam owned more than twenty palaces, he had his food inspected and carefully prepared, while he had his chef's cook three elaborate meals a day. He made it look to appear as if all of them were up and running, so that anytime he could be anywhere. Ruthless ruler remains in hiding as the manhunt begins. He is seen only on audio tapes released to Arab television networks in which his voice was unrecognizable. As the troops come closer to him, he continues to hide. On December 13th-2003, about nine miles outside of Saddam's hometown of Tikrit, U.S. soldiers capture Saddam, who is hiding in a "spider hole" the entrance of the hole camouflaged with bricks and dirt was near a compound of ramshackle buildings. He doesn't resist arrest as he is uncovered. He is dishelved and unkempt in his appearance. He has a long bushy graying beard and matted hair. He was found unharmed, talkative and cooperative. His twenty-four year "hellish reign comes to a close. He can take his rightful place right along side of Hitler, Stalin and any other brutal dictators. Iraqi people are well on their way to freedom as quoted by Rumsfeld. Our president has promised the Iraqi's that this day would come as the aforementioned name Iraqi Freedom becomes realized. Still the war continues on as a fight for freedom becomes all too real. With war there are always casualties. The faces of the fallen haunt our lives. We have to bury our own. The media reminds each and every day the real truth of the brutality of war, crossing enemy lines, our fight for freedom in times of war. Please continue to pray for our service men and women as they experience what we only see on the news, and pray that our president will make the right decisions when we are called into battle. The good news is that a day of reckoning has come for Saddam, on November 6th-2006; Saddam is sentenced to die a hanging death of his war crimes. He and two of his co-defendants are facing the gallows. Saddam's half-brother and former intelligence chief are sentenced for crimes against humanity. In one of the most highly publicized and heavily reported trials, Saddam and his accusers were brought to trial. The iron-fisted dictator, Saddam shouted out "long live the people and death to their enemies" as the verdict was read. Saddam's chief lawyer condemned that the trial was a farce, claiming the verdict was planned. The defense attorneys would appeal in thirty days. The death sentences automatically go to a nine-judge appeals panel, which has unlimited time to review the case. If the verdicts and sentences are upheld, the executions must be carried out within thirty days. (As reported by Fox News). There are ramifications of Saddam's sentencing with the Islamic leaders giving warning that executing Saddam could inflame those who revile the U.S.., undermining the policy in the Middle East and inspiring terrorists. In Saddam's hometown of Tikrit, a thousand people defied the curfew and carried pictures of Saddam's favorite son through the streets. Saddam "by our souls, by our blood we sacrifice for you, and Saddam your name shakes America. There is security fears, Saddam's supporters had threatened bloodshed if he was convicted at the end of the nine month trial, and U.S. and Iraqi forces stepped up security Saturday in a country that is in a constant state of marital law. Military patrols were increased and a main Baghdad bridge that carries traffic past the Green Zone has been blocked off. Saddam Hussein's trial is a milestone in the Iraqi people's efforts to replace the rule of a tyrant with the rule of law. It's a major achievement for Iraq's young democracy and its constitutional government. Saddam's trial heard from a hundred witnesses and brought him face to face with his victims as they recounted the crimes committed against them. The victims of the regime have received a measure of the justice, that many thought would never come. The verdict absolutely proves that Iraq has an independent judiciary that operates fairly and openly. This is a verdict of a whole dark era, which became past history like the eras of other dictators who had a rise to power only to fall. On December 29-2006 justice is served Saddam Hussein is put to death by hanging. Happy New Year! Iraq a free nation.

Proverbs 10:29 The way of the Lord is strength to the upright: but destruction shall be to the workers of iniquity.

Getting Orders
and Saying Goodbye

The Saunders Story Of North Folk, Virginia

The leaves are gently falling, as autumn arrives. Their colors so vividly vibrant, in hues of burgundy, gold and orange. The smell of fall is in the air. I pull in the drive way as my children run out to greet me. Cameron is four, Amber is five, and my wife, Tonya lovingly watches them as they run into my arms. I pick them up and hug them, as they excitedly hug my neck. Daddy's home, daddy's home. Tonya greets me with a kiss. We walk into the house and decide to go to dinner at our favorite restaurant, little Italy. We talk about my day at work. I am a production foreman for a computer software company. The job wants us to relocate to open in another state. Tonya looks saddened as I tell her that this is a possibility, but of course I said no. We get the kids ready and go to dinner. We get to the restaurant, get seated, and hold hands to pray together. Our dinner arrives and we enjoy what little time we have had together lately. After dinner we decide to hit the local department store, and shop for fall clothes for Cameron and Amber. Amber is quite the little shopper as she pulls clothes from the rack and hands them to her mom. Cameron doesn't like to shop; he hides under the clothing rack as we shop. Cameron is promised an ice-cream cone if he can behave just a little longer. Daddy says "Cameron, young man do you want time-out?" Cameron straightens up when daddy raises his voice. We check out and go to the ice-cream store. Daddy reprimands Cameron for his misbehavior. He has four minutes of time-out, and then he can answer why he misbehaved. He apologizes and is forgiven. Now we can enjoy our treat. When we get home, it is bath time and bedtime; we pray with our children and tuck them in. Tonya and I have a further discussion about my job, I reassure her that I will quit before I have to travel again and be away from my wife and children. I have some vacation time, so we will go away. We can go to Tennessee and see the Great Smoky Mountains. Let's sleep on it and we will discuss it this weekend. Tonya and I pray together and ask God for guidance in all of life's decisions. I go to work, and Tonya starts her daily routine with breakfast, packing lunches, and getting Amber to school. Cameron is in pre-k and goes in the afternoon. Today is a field trip for Cameron to the apple orchard; I will be riding with him on the bus. He is so excited, but would have liked for daddy to come to. "Maybe next time Cameron daddy can." My little blonde haired blue eyed cherub looks just like his dad, and has his mannerisms. We board the bus and I am appointed watch of two of Cameron's friends, Colton and Connor. We get to the orchard and go on a hay ride. We then taste the warm rich cider that gives us a feeling of warmth. We sit at a picnic table and eat our lunches, the kids can then have time to run and play, we go on a short hike, board the buses and head home. We pick Amber up from school and head home to prepare dinner. Cameron is asleep in the car, and we get home and start homework, while I put dinner on. I am setting the table and daddy is home. "Hello dear I love you." He comes in with a dozen roses. hidden behind his back. He has a gift for Amber and Cameron to. "What is the occasion?" I got a pay raise and wanted to celebrate. "How wonderful, life is so sweet." We have dinner, tell the kids about our upcoming trip to the mountains, and enjoy a movie in our family room. Pray with our children as this is our daily routine. Time swiftly marches on and the holidays are upon us as we prepare for the Thanksgiving holiday. We will have family over and have buffet style dinner complete with reading bible scripture and bible discussion. I am so grateful for family. God truly blesses the unity of family. On Thanksgiving Day I am up early to taste the delicious turkey Tonya is so famous for making. She is up mixing and stirring and preparing for our family's feast. The smell of pumpkin pie wafts to me from my easy chair, tempting my senses. Cameron and Amber busily play and wait in anticipation for our company to arrive. The time has come for our company to arrive and my mom and dad come in, and Tonya's parents and sister come to our house. When everyone has taken their seat, I pray the blessing on our meal, we go around the table and everyone tells what they are thankful for. It is a very good meal, and we read scripture before eating our dessert. As with most family's we retreat to the living room and watch TV, while my wife and the women clean up. We rest for the remainder of the day. The shopping frenzy begins the day after. There are many gifts to get. The widows in our church, the angel tree, the needy families and the children's home are the ones we purpose to get first. We have taught our children to follow Jesus example of servitude. While I sleep in, Tonya and the children rush off to the stores for the many sales. I roll out of bed to get some coffee and breakfast. Time goes by and before I know it my family is home. We pack for our trip and will be leaving at 5:00 am. The alarm clock rings and we sleepily rise out of bed. Cameron and Amber are already stirring. We hit the highway, while the children fall asleep in the car. Tonya joins them in a restful state. I have time to think and meditate. I have been watching the news as things have heated up in the Middle East. In a couple of days I will tell my family that I am going to Iraq, but not now. My wife looks so peaceful and my children look very content, as I ponder the thought of leaving them, even for a little while. It is time to stop for gas and breakfast. Tonya awakens and the children are ready to get out and stretch. We eat breakfast, pray for traveling mercies and head back out. Many hours later we arrive at our hotel. The hotel has a heated pool, so we gather our things check in and head to the pool. We enjoy our time together and head for our room. The next morning we start our day and sight see. We go to the Great Smoky Mountains, we shop and walk and hike. The mountains are magnificent, such a beautiful place to visit. Looking at nature and feeling God has created all that we see. We stay at this beautiful piece of heaven for five more days. The time has come to get ready to leave; we stop and take many more pictures to remember this family vacation. We arrive home and collect the week's worth of mail. I sit in my easy chair as the hustle and bustle of putting things away from our trip. I pick up the envelop I dreaded to read, with tears in my eyes, I read the notice from the United States Marine Corps. Division. Corporal R.S. you are to report for duty and departure one week from December 27-2006 @ 1:00 pm. I cannot contain my emotions and step outside while my family is busy. I will plan a dinner with my wife and break the news gently. Tonya is such an understanding person, she will be fine. I worry about my children and how they will handle my going away. We talk about it at dinner; Tonya can hardly hold back the tears, she to was going to surprise me with a new addition to our family. I am so overwhelmed and happy at this wonderful news. Tonya, we will tell the kids later in the week. Sounds good honey, God will help us through this trial. The time comes to gently tell our children daddy won't be coming home for awhile. Cameron has a temper tantrum, and Amber sobs at already missing daddy. We plan an outing everyday during the holidays; we take day trips and spend as much quality time as we can fit in our schedules. We go to our first ob/gyn appointment and find out the due date for our little miracle. Dr. Greenberg has confirmed August 21st as the blessed event. We talk about setting up the nursery, what color scheme, a name; there are so many things to do before daddy leaves. We decide on Danielle if she's a girl and Richard if he's a boy. We will decorate Noah's ark theme. The next few weeks we are busily getting the nursery ready. We are Christmas shopping, and putting up border, organizing and making room for our new arrival. We decorate for Christmas, pick out a tree. It is our family tradition to decorate our tree as a family. When the tree is decorated, we then sing songs to Jesus, and thank Him for our blessings. It looks like a white

Christmas is in the forecast. We turn in for the night, and awaken early to a velvety blanket of snow. The snow glistens as the light of day peeks through. We take our places and daddy appoints Cameron as his little helper. Cameron will give the presents out. Amber will help put the wrap in the bag. Mommy is on the camera crew. She will be videoing this Christmas as a cherished memory. Everyone excitedly opens their gifts. When the gifts are opened it is breakfast together. The next few days I have leave from work, I spend every waking moment with my children, cherishing their smiles, wiping away tears. I have been slowly packing, but time is drawing near.

We ring in the New Year with all of our family at our house. We make a memory book that the children can have when they question when daddy is coming home. Tonya drives me to the airport and we hug and kiss and huddle as a family. The time has come when my plane arrives. I look as my family leaves, with a hard lump in my throat; I put my luggage on the conveyor belt and try not to think about my tour of duty. There are two-three hour lay over and one delay. I call to tell my family goodnight. I know it will be several days until I am able to hear their voices. I hold their pictures to my chest as I pray for God to take care of them for me. The plane ride seems like an eternity. Upon arrival to Iraq, there is another pit stop before I go to the location where I will be living. It is a short ride to meet with another person to discuss our project mission. I meet with my appointed platoon. We bunk down for the night and awake to the sound of missiles in the distant. We put on our gear and load our ammunition and plan what area we will patrol today. The weather is getting colder so we layer our clothing, put on our knapsack and go into enemy territory. The sound of gunfire and grenades echo in our ears. The sound of the screaming as someone is ambushed is all too real. We are not a welcome candidate for a war torn country. I call home and am given just a few minutes to reconnect with my life back home. All is well, and time is swiftly passing as the baby is coming quicker than August. On July 4th, Richard Allen is brought into the world, and I am thousands of miles away, but Tonya has taped his first cries for me. We cry together and I tell my son how much his daddy loves him. It will be nine and a half months before I will get to meet my son. Tonya sends me pictures of him on my cell phone. The three of them are a real strength to me to get back home to them. The time gets closer and closer and I am anxiously awaiting my flight plans. The final day has come to return to American soil and the beautiful hills of Virginia. In less than twenty four hours I will be in my wife's arms and our family will be reunited. I get to the airport and see in the distance my family who look so different than I remember. Tears are welling up in my eyes and clouding my vision. I cannot walk fast enough to get to them. We run into each other's arms and huddle. I gaze at my beautiful little boy God has blessed us with. Tonya puts him in my arms and he says

Da dad. What! music to my ears. Tonya and I embrace and kiss and cry together. Cameron and Amber can't stop smiling. They are so happy to see their daddy. Cameron says, "Daddy is my hero." We go home and try to get back to normal life. The next few months are tough for daddy. He has nightmares of being in enemy territory, the doctor has said he has post traumatic stress syndrome, we continue to pray for him and help him through this. The faces of war are vividly imprinted in his mind, yet he tries to retain a normal life. Daddy holds Richard's hands and helps him to learn to walk. Daddy is able to go on field trips with Cameron. Amber is in dance class and daddy will be there for her. Our family circle is complete. Amber has been asking questions about Jesus. We have explained to her that He died for our sins in our place." Mommy can Jesus live in my heart to?" "Yes, Amber just ask Him to forgive you as a sinner." She bows her little head and prays for Jesus forgiveness. Daddy walks in the room and kneels and prays with his daughter. Her heart is tender and she accepts Jesus as her savior. This is such a blessing for our family. We gather together and read John 3:16 For God so loved the world; that He gave His only begotten son that whosoever believeth in Him shall not perish but have everlasting life. "What does everlasting mean daddy?" "It means for ever and ever, never to end, just as a circle has no beginning and no end it is complete for eternity." "We will live with Jesus forever." Amber smiles and hugs mommy and daddy. Daddy gives Amber her first bible with the date she became a child of the king. The next day is Sunday and we announce the good news to our church family. Everyone is happy and hugs Amber. Our pastor prays for her and asks Gods blessing in her life. We have a special luncheon at the fellowship hall. We stay for awhile and head home. Next week our youngest will be dedicated to the Lord. It is hard to believe how quickly our children change and grow up. Children are a gift from God given to us to borrow for awhile. We must model Christian behavior in front of them and teach them about the love of their heavenly father. We continue to face trials in our lives, but depend on Jesus to see us through. We are in a spiritual battle, but with Gods help we will win. Please pray for our family as we raise our children in the admonition of the Lord. Thank you for your prayers and thank you for taking the time to get to know our family unit. May God bless you and shine His glorious light in your lives. Sincerely, the Saunders.

Proverbs 22:6 Train up a child in the way he should go; and when he is old he will not depart from it.

The Connors Story Of Raleigh, North Carolina

The temperatures are quickly heating up in the south. In Raleigh, North Carolina the sun is always hotter. K. C. moved to the south because of the southern hospitality. While K.C and his wife Lori and their twin girls had searched to find a dream home he longed for the mountains. The day that the realtor had called about the house, excitement had already been building and it was a go. They would build a log cabin in the woods. It was all set, their house had sold without a hitch, and this truly was a blessing. K.C.'s family lived right there in Raleigh and Lori's friend from college lived within ten miles. " God answers prayers" was K.C and Lori's reply. K.C. worked for Geo tech as a superintendent and was able to relocate. K.C. also had a second job, which was most important to serve our country as a chief petty officer in the navy. His grandfather and father and uncle had all served their country. K.C. wanted to follow in his dad's footsteps and at a very young age he would have interest in the service as a navy man. He always asked for military toys and would pretend to be in the battle zone with some of his friends. Then all through school he couldn't wait to give an oath to join the navy. When graduation came he had earned a scholarship and went to school for technical engineering. He graduated with honors and gave his oath to serve his country. He smiles as he remembers his days of boot camp. The many lessons of life you learn as a " green horn," you think you know everything, and try to prove yourselves only to be knocked down to size by your superiors. Man do you get in shape or pay the consequences for disobedience. After the dilemma of boot camp you are ready to try out what you have learned. I went to work on the naval ship and learned to get along with my buddy, Randall, who taught me how to become the man I always wanted to be. Randall had a sense of humor and that is what helped him to stay straight. I learned a lot along the way and wanted to be in charge someday. So I started doing my best and impressed my sergeant. I quickly moved up in rank and became chief petty officer. I passed on some of my earlier lessons to my men under me. I would pray to my heavenly father, and he always gave me wisdom about things. My wife Lori has a full time position at our local bank, she is head teller. She is a great mom to our girls. Our girls are Haley and Hannah. They are very good natured and have their mother's meek, gentle spirit. They have my sense of humor, so I would say they're evenly balanced. We are packing our things to relocate to the mountains. We have our plans for our new home and we have located our property. We have to find a church close by so we can worship there. We are renting a u-haul and taking everything we own, we hope in one trip. Lori can relocate to another bank in Raleigh. The time comes and we go to settlement for our house. We are leaving in the next few days. We have our things in marked boxes for what room it will go into. The girls are excited to spend time with their grandparents. We head out for our trip, stop for gas and something to eat. We have brought other healthy snack foods for the in between stops. Lori always packs nutritious foods and has taught our girls to eat healthy. We have pictures of our new home that was sent to us before we left. We have what colors we picked out, for which room. We have two fire places and two lofts for the girls. We have a great room and a family room; we have a wrap around porch to watch those beautiful sun sets. Seems that life can't get any better. Upon our arrival we are surprised when we see three cars on our new driveway. We walk into our new home and people jump out to surprise us. My mom and dad and Lori's friends have gotten together and planned this for us. "Welcome home Connor's." What! an awesome surprise. There is food, fun, and fellowship. We ask the Lord's blessing on our food. We unpack and reminisce and say our goodbyes for the night. We bunk down for the night in our sleeping bags and pillows; we say our prayers and thank God for our safe trip. The next morning the sun is up, and the smell of bacon teases my pallet. The girls want their mom's famous vanilla flap jacks, so we enjoy our breakfast on our new front porch. There are so many things to do when you detour from one way of living to the next. The girls help their mom clean up the kitchen while I unpack the outside toys. Lori is unpacking one room at a time as Haley and Hannah put their things away in their new rooms. The grandparents come back to help set up house. The family bible is placed on the table in the family room, where there is a family altar. K.C. will unpack and set up his garage. He will also unpack his riding toy to mow the acreage. The mountains are so serene and peaceful. This is a carefree life. The beauty that God has created will in a sense take your breath away. I only have a few more days before I am to start my new job. Lori has taken a few more days to make sure everything is done and to register the girls at their new school. She will meet with the faculty and take the girls for a tour of their school. They will not be in the same class, but will be across the hall from one another. The field trips and special times will often bring them together. Both are very excited to meet new friends and join dance class, just like at home. Lori takes them school shopping after meeting with the teacher, and getting the supplies list. She has offered an occasional Friday to be in the girl's room as a helper. This is a very welcome idea. This school loves parent involvement and encourages child parent participation. There is a student of the week program, where one special child per class, per grade, gets recognized and can earn a special award. Both girls will actively compete for this. On the way home we stop and sign up for dance class. This auditorium is gigantic. The same outfits can be worn, but another type of shoes has to be bought. They have rehearsal every Tuesday and Thursday night. Excitement fills the air as the thought of spending two nights in dance and meeting new friends becomes a reality. "I can't wait until we can dance for grand mom and poppy, replied Haley. " Yeah and daddy" replied Hannah. Hannah always tries to please daddy first, she is his little helper, but daddy encourages Haley and loves both of his princesses equally. We leave to go home and pick up dinner at a local restaurant. Daddy is sitting on the front porch, resting and relaxing. He has set the table for our dinner. We put Christian music on and pray over our food. We talk about our day and take the time for each other. Time for each other should never be rushed, take time to listen for time passes by swiftly and the winds of time can change and we might not have another opportunity to communicate freely and show our love for each other. We clean up after dinner and just enjoy the time we are spending together. Tomorrow daddy goes to his new job. New boss, new employees, new rules. Let us pray for God's will in our lives. We bow in perfect submission to our Lord Jesus and hold hands as we ask for His will be done. Time to turn in for bed. The next morning at 6:00 a.m. I get up shower, get dressed and start my day. Breakfast is ready before I leave, and my lunch is packed. The girls kiss me goodbye and I am off to work. Today is Haley and Hannah's first day at their new school. Haley dresses up, Hannah dresses down. These two are as different as night and day, Haley has her new skirt outfit, while Hannah has jeans and a tee shirt. So much for dressing alike. Even as young as four they fussed to look alike, so we gave them their own sense of styles. Haley is prim and proper like her mom; Hannah is rugged like her dad. Lori gets their lunches packed and drives them to school. She stays with them until they leave for class. She kisses them goodbye and goes home and meditates and prays. Lori puts on music and straightens her house up; she has plenty of time before she is to pick the girls up. She takes out her crock-pot and marinades her roast for dinner. She peels and cuts the potatoes in cubes, adding in her spices for flavoring. While her dinner is cooking she makes the girls favorite dessert, rice crispy treats. She melts the butter and adds in the marshmallows.

Lori walks outside and takes in the beauty of this wonderful place. The mountains atop their property give off a fog like appearance, with whitish circles, resembling snow capped mountains. She goes in and checks out the simmering roast. She adds in her carrots and dinner is completed. Now for the laundry piled high, she folds and irons her husband's work shirts and uniform pants for his job. Much time is passed and before she knows it, it is time to pick up the girls. The girls spot her and come running to tell her about their day." I like my teachers", Haley replies. "I have a new friend mommy who sits beside me in all my classes." "Her name is Charity." "That is wonderful girls, I am so glad you are adjusting, just like I knew you would." We get home and daddy is pulling in the driveway. We meet him and he gives us hugs and kisses and tells us how much he loves us. We sit down to dinner and talk about our day, daddy asks mommy to pray. "Dear father, thank you for my family, I pray protection around them, I pray for our food, thy will be done." Like all good things come to an end, so do the times we have together. Daddy received an official letter and a call from The United States Naval Academy. He knew he could be called in anytime, but didn't expect it to come so soon after relocating and getting settled in. There is a moment of silence as he tells us to save a place at our table until he is to return. He will be leaving in three days. He is called to Baghdad. We pray together again, this time for daddy's safety and his safe return. It is time for bed and we put our children to bed and retire to bed ourselves. "Lori, I know you can handle things, as soon as I can get back here I will." I am doing this for Uncle Robert." Remember how numb we were when those terrorist plotted to hit the twin towers and uncle Robert was working that morning, he almost called in sick, but was entirely too dedicated to do that." "And do you remember when he was sick and we prayed for him and he accepted Jesus as his personal savior, I am so thankful he didn't die in his sins." "It is duty to first my savior and my country to protect my loved ones and protect the freedom we have." "Here is my plane information and tickets and departure time. " Do you think my angel girls will be okay?" "They are strong and trust Jesus to see us through these trials we all have to face." "My parents can go with us to the airport, and can stay with you and the girls for awhile. The day arrives and it is curtain call for the next stage of my life. We drive to the airport, holding onto the memories of our lives, while the fleeting thought of missing you burns into my heart and very soul. We say our goodbyes and return home to an empty nest, without daddy. We try to go with our not so normal lives. But the silence of what once filled our home is a distant memory. We anxiously await his call, and run to get the phone every time it rings. The next night after dinner and homework is complete, daddy calls, his voice sounds so faint, like he is a million miles away, he is very happy to talk to us. He sounds very optimistic like it won't be long before he is back with us. K.C. can hear the enemy fire, and the truck that has burst into flames where an enemy has rigged the truck with explosives. Some nights he doesn't sleep but for a few minutes while another soldier is keeping watch. The conditions that some soldiers face while going into combat would blow our minds. The enemy is always within range, and always trying to be one step ahead of you to trip you up, like the way chess is played. Months pass by as time continues to fly. The girls back home have had their first dance recital; mommy has taken many pictures for daddy. Daddy calls again to tell us they are sending in more troops and he can return home in a few months. I can hardly believe how quickly time flies, he has been there for almost a year. Lori has her own bible class of women that she is teaching on a weekly basis. The girls have joined a swimming class. They have made many new friends. Life goes on. We have to learn to roll with the punches. The day comes when daddy is due home; we are so excited and can hardly wait to see him again. We arrive at the airport looking our very best, with pictures in hand and daddy's favorite dessert, brownies with caramel, which the girls made to surprise him. The plane lands and he runs to us, tears streaming down his face. Hugs can last forever or so it seems. The mayor has heard of soldiers coming home and meets us at the airport to offer his gratitude, shakes hands and congratulates him on his safe return. We get home and enjoy dinner and the brownies for daddy. This is another success story, though some are not as successful as others. Thank you for taking the time to get to know the Connors family; I thank you for your prayers, and your continued support of our troops who can't be home to enjoy their families. They will have a much greater reward for the lives they are protecting. We pray for Gods protection for our fellow service men and women. I pray for freedom of religion in our world. I pray God will cease enemy fire. I pray for the Iraqi people to extinguish hate in their hearts for Americans. God can melt a heart of stone. Continue to pray as our soldiers cross into enemy territory that they will be protected by

Gods shield and He will quench the fiery darts of the wicked one. Evil never wins; grace and mercy will always reign. Jesus will rule and reign in our hearts and our lives if we just learn to trust and obey His word.

Praising Him for eternity! Sincerely, the Connors

John 4:24 God is a spirit; and they that worship Him must worship Him in spirit and in truth.

Foreign Soil

Iraq History Of Land And People

The definition of foreign is: not native, located outside a specific district; province etc. To be sent outside the realm of comfort can be very stressful in its self. To go into a war zone, in a country that has been programmed by a dictator to hate Americans, can be most dangerous and the bottom line, lots of casualties. Let us learn about the background of Iraq and Iran and the Palestinian state. To know the land and its people and the geographic location can help us to understand its origin and purpose. First we will speak of Iraq, Iraq is twice the size of Idaho, a triangle of mountains, desert and fertile river valley is bounded on the east by Iran, on the west by Syria and Jordan, on the north by Turkey, and on the south by Saudi Arabia and Kuwait. The country has arid desert land west of the Euphrates, a broad central valley between the Euphrates and the Tigris, and mountains in the northeast. Iraq's land area is 167,566 sq mi, population 26,783,383, capital and largest city is Baghdad 6,777,300 (metro area). Iraq's history, from the earliest times was known as Mesopotamia- the land between the rivers-for it embraces a large part of the alluvial plains of the Euphrates and Tigris rivers. The land became the center of the ancient Babylonian and Assyrian empires sometime after 2000 B.C. Mesopotamia was conquered by Cyrus the great of Persia in 538 B.C. and by Alexander in 331 B.C. After an Arab conquest in 637-640, Baghdad became the capital. The country was cruelly pillaged by the Mongols in 1258, and during the 16th, 17th, and 18th centuries was the object of repeated Turkish-Persian competition. Britain occupied most of Mesopotamia in World War I and was given a mandate over the area in 1920. The British renamed the area Iraq and recognized it as a kingdom in 1922. The monarchy achieved full independence in 1932. During World War II, Britain again occupied Iraq because of its pro-Axis stance in the initial years of the war. Iraq became a charter member of the Arab League in 1945, and Iraqi troops took part in the Arab invasion of the Palestine in 1948. From earliest times Iraq began to form alliances with Communist countries, and Iraq was known economic disparities between rich and poor. Iraq, a leading producer of oil in the world used its oil revenues to develop one of the strongest military forces in the region. On July 16th, 1979, Saddam Hussein was second in command, whose regime steadily developed an international reputation for human rights abuses, repression and terrorism. Saddam imposed authoritarian rule in an effort to end the decades of political instability that followed World War II. He was a fearful dictator that people feared for their lives if they went against his regime. In 1991, the UN set up a northern no-fly zone to protect Iraq's Kurdish population, in 1992, a southern no-fly zone was established as a buffer between Iraq and Kuwait and to protect Shiites. The UN

Security Council imposed sanctions that barred Iraq from selling oil except in exchange for food and medicine. The sanctions failed to crush their leader Saddam, but caused catastrophic suffering among its people- the country's infrastructure was in ruins, malnutrition and disease, and the infant mortality rate skyrocketed. Now that we know a little more about Iraq as our enemy, we can be more cautious and take the necessary precautions needed to protect our loved ones.

Psalm 2:1 Why do the heathen rage, and the people imagine a vain thing?

Iran

History Of Land And People

Iran, a Middle Eastern country shares borders with Iraq, Turkey, Armenia, Afghanistan, Azerbaijan, Turkmenistan, and Pakistan. Iran is south of the Caspian Sea and north of the Persian Gulf and is three times the size of Arizona. The Elburz Mountains in the north rise to 18,603 ft at Mount Damavend. From northwest to southwest, the country is crossed by a dessert 800 mi. The capital and largest city of Iran is Teheran, 7,796,257. The land area is 631,659 sq mi. The estimated population is 68,688,433. In 1500s B.C. the region now called Iran was occupied by the Medes and the Persians, until the Persian king Cyrus the Great overthrew the Medes and became ruler of the Persian Empire. Persia had become an international scientific and cultural center by the mid 800s. In the 12th

Century it was invaded by the Mongols. The dominant religion became the Shiite Islam, followed and then was replaced by Qajar Dynasty (1794-1925). During the

Qajar Dynasty, the British and Russians fought for economic control of the area, and during World War I,

Iran's neutrality did not stop it from becoming a battlefield for British and Russian troops. In 1921, a coup brought Reza Kahn to power; he did much to modernize the country and abolished all foreign extraterritorial rights. In World War II, the country's pro-Axis allegiance led to

Anglo-Russian occupation of Iran in 1941. Iran's history has much significance with it being allies with Iraq. An Islamic theocracy was established and the Islamic traditions were to urge women to return to wearing the veil; banned western music and alcohol and mixed bathing; closed universities, shut down the media and eliminated political parties. Iran's natural resources are: coal, natural gas, petroleum, copper, iron, ore, lead, manganese, chromium, zinc and sulfur. Exports: petroleum 80%fruits and nuts, carpets and chemical and petrochemical products. Imports: capital goods, food stuffs and other consumer goods, technical services, industrial raw materials, and military supplies. Major trading partners: Italy, South Africa, China, Japan, Germany, France, South Korea, Taiwan, Turkey, Netherlands, UAE, and Russia. Agriculture: sugar beets, fruits, nuts, cotton, wheat, rice, other grains, dairy products, wool and caviar. Religions: 98% Islamic, Jewish, Christian, Zoroastrian, and Baha'i 2%. Languages spoken: Persian and Persian dialects 58%, Turkic and Turkic dialects 26% Kurdish 9%, Luri 2%, Baloch 2% Turkmen 2% other 1%. Ethnicity/ race: Persian 51%, Kurd 7%, Arab 3%, Lur 2%, Turkmen 2%. International disputes: Iran protests Afghanistan's limiting flow of dammed tributaries to the Helmand River in periods of drought; Iraq's lack of a maritime boundary with Iran prompts jurisdiction disputes beyond the mouth of the Shatt al

Arab in the Persian Gulf; Iran and UAE engage in direct talks and solicit Arab League support to resolve disputes over Iran's occupation of Tunb Islands and Abu Musa Island; Iran stands alone among littoral states in insisting upon a division of the Caspian Sea into five equal sectors. Transportation: Ports and Harbors, Airports, Waterways, Railways and Highways. Now we know a little bit of history for another of our allies, Iran, they too do not like military involvement in their country. They too are the enemy.

They're another axis of evil, we need to be aware of they're every move.

Psalm 60:12 Through God we shall do valiantly: for He it is that shall tread down our enemies.

Palestinian State

The History Of Land And People

The West Bank is located to the east of Israel and the west of Jordan. The Gaza Strip is located between Israel and Egypt on the Mediterranean coast. The history of the proposed modern Palestinian state began with the British mandate of Palestine. Britain controlled the region from September 29th, 1923, until May 14th-1948, but by 1947 Britain had appealed to the UN to solve the complex problem of competing Palestinian and Jewish claims to the land. The UN proposed in August 1947 by dividing Palestine into a Jewish state, an Arab state and a small international zone. Arabs rejected the idea, and as soon as Britain pulled out of Palestine in 1948, neighboring Arab nations invaded, with intent on crushing the newly declared state of Israel. Israel emerged victorious, affirming its sovereignty. The remaining areas of Palestine were divided between Transjordan (now Jordan) which annexed the West Bank and Egypt, which gained control of the Gaza Strip. The largest cities: Gaza 1,331,600 Hebron, 137,000 Nablus, 115,400. Languages: Hebrew, English and Arabic. Religions: West Bank: Islam

75%, Jewish 17% Christian and other 8%, Gaza Strip: Islam 98.7%. Agriculture: vegetables, beef, olives, citrus, and dairy products. Industries: generally small family businesses that produce: textiles, soap, cement, olive-wood carvings, and mother- of- pearl souvenirs; the Israelis have established some small-scale, modern industries in the settlements and industrial centers. Natural resources: natural gas, and arable land. Exports: flowers, textiles, citrus, olives, fruit, vegetables, and limestone. Imports: consumer goods, food, and construction materials. Major trading partners: West Bank, Egypt, Israel, Jordan and Gaza Strip. Transportation: Highways; Gaza Strip Railways,

Ports and harbors, Airports, and West Bank. International disputes: Gaza strip and the West Bank is Israeli- occupied with current status subject to the Israeli-Palestinian Interim Agreement- permanent status to be determined through further negotiation. On September 13, 1993, Arafat and Israeli Prime Minister Yitzak Rabin signed the historic "Declaration of Principles." As part of the agreement Israel pulled out of the Gaza Strip and Jericho in the West Bank in 1994. The Palestinian Authority, with Arafat as its elected leader, took control of the newly non-Israeli-occupied areas, assuming all governmental duties. In the years that followed fighting continued and intensive negotiations remained deadlocked over Israeli-occupied east Jerusalem. The U.S. would not recognize an independent Palestinian state until Arafat was replaced. Arafat agreed to political reforms: his government to the disillusionment of many Palestinians was rife with corruption. Just like a rise to power with Arafat, he to fell from his dictator throne. Yasir Arafat died on November

10th, marking the end of an era in Palestinian affairs. There is still no peace for the Palestinian people as they continue to want peace with Israel. They want right to their land and want a cease fire from violence. Continue to pray that there will be peace in Palestine. The Gaza Strip is a biblical location mentioned in the bible. Events in the Middle East are prophesized to take place when Jesus returns.

Psalm 121:1 I will lift up mine eyes unto the hills; from whence cometh my help.

New Horizons

The Story Of Airman Mi Of Montana

I am from the mid-west in the beautiful state of Montana. Born and raised there, the landscaping is picture perfect. Montana, known as big sky, open land, majestic mountains and friendly people combine to make Montana the "Treasure State." My family grew up in Great Falls, I am one of four, and I have an older brother and two younger sisters. My dad worked as a dentist, my mom as an accountant at Department of Transportation. I played sports and my sisters both took dance class and drama. Growing up was fun, we could explore our environment and go to historical parks and hike trails. When I got out of school I was unsure which direction my life would go, I had interest in engineering and would take classes at our local college. Before I graduated from college, a friend asked me to join the service with him; we were the best of friends so I decided to join the guard. I was gone only two weekends a month and we both were in together. I liked the guard, and decided to enlist in the United States Air force. I finished my college while in the Air force. I would be sent to Antonio Texas for boot camp. My best friend,

Garret also got to go with me. It was a grueling experience of quickly growing up to manhood. We were the new kids on the block, and learned quickly the ways of the world. While on leave to go home one week, I was jogging in the park and met the most beautiful girl I had ever seen. Her green eyes sparkled, and her hair was long and beautiful. I mustered up a quick hello. She said she was taking a break from college, and decided to walk in the park. We sat and talked and she agreed to meet me later for dinner." I will pick you up at 6:00, Kara." I was so excited that I got pulled over and given a warning for speeding. I pulled in the driveway and mom was outside in her flower bed, " Why are you smiling son?" "I got a date tonight mom." "That is wonderful son, have fun." The next three hours seemed to go by so slowly. Finally the time is come to get ready. I dress in my new civilian clothes, put on cologne and head out the door. I stop and pick up a rose. Kara is patiently waiting to see me when I pull up to her house. I give her the rose and she goes inside to put it in a vase. She looks more ravishing than she did in the park earlier. We go to a local restaurant and order dinner and talk. We have candlelight on our table, it is the perfect evening. The remainder of the time I am home we spend time together. Kara is interested in seeing more of me, I tell her I will be home again for the holidays. When I get back to the base, we call each other and stay in touch. On a weekend I get a call that Kara has come to visit, I have a weekend pass. We go sight seeing in Texas. In a few weeks I will be home. We say our goodbyes and promise to keep in touch. I constantly remember her scent and her very lovely way of that warm fuzzy feeling we get when were in love. Could this be happening to me? I got to find out if she feels the same way I do. The next day she has sent me a letter. The letter is sealed with a kiss. She said she has fallen head over heals in love with me. Next week I will be home, back in her arms and we can talk about the next serious stage of our lives. The day I am due home she meets me at the airport. I run into her arms and we embrace and kiss. This is a kodak moment. I have an idea I will shop for her alone to pick out an engagement ring for Kara and surprise her at the park where we met. I will ask her father at dinner Christmas Eve for her hand in marriage. My mom and dad will be ecstatic at my settling down. I will invite my parents out to dinner, and introduce Kara, and we will tell them together about our decision to marry. The next day I take a ride to the jewelry store to find the perfect ring. I look at five or six before I decide on the one. It is a round solitaire with baguettes. She will love it. I finish my purchase and put this treasure in my pocket. When I get home I put it up. Christmas Eve is another special day, it is my favorite time of the year, streets decorated, houses lit up and in the air there is a feeling of Christmas. Tonight after dinner I will ask Bob, Kara's dad to join me in the living room and ask him for his daughter's hand in marriage. He is very happy to join me and happily says yes to my question. Then we have dessert and play music and exchange a gift. Kara loves the necklace I bought her. I love the photo album she bought me to cherish our pictures as we begin our lives together. Christmas morning I wake up early and our family exchanges gifts, mom makes my favorite breakfast, hash browns, eggs, and bacon. Later I pick Kara up and we plan a lunch in the park, where I will pop the question. I spread out a blanket as we get our lunch set up, I get on bended knee, take out the velvet box, and ask Kara "will you marry me?" Her response was "I will." She put the ring on and it sparkled the same excitement her green eyes had sparkled the day we met. What! a moment in time. I was the happiest man alive. We rushed home and told her parents, but kept the excitement until the dinner with my parents. I reserved a table in our favorite restaurant, seated my fiancée and my parents. We ordered our food and I told my parents they were dining with their new daughter-in law to be. "That is wonderful news." We talked about a date to marry; we talked about the wedding party, arrangements etc. Time quickly marches on, and the time is soon upon you as you make the final arrangements for the big day. We have a big wedding planned and a honey moon in St. Thomas. The day has finally arrived and I am standing at the alter awaiting my beautiful bride. The music begins and here comes the bride. She is more elegant and beautiful, she has a glow. We join hands repeat our vows and are joined in holy matrimony. Pictures are taken and we are off to celebrate at our reception. I dance the first dance with my new bride. She dances to Butterfly Kisses with her dad. I dance a song with my mom. She has been crying, she is happy for us. We cut our cake, mingle with our friends, family, and acquaintances. Open our gifts and get ready to go to our destination. We will be leaving tomorrow morning to catch a plane. We say our thank you, goodbyes and head out to our awaiting limo. In the morning we go to the airport to go to our destination in St. Thomas. We arrive, find our room and spend time getting to know each other. The beaches are white sand. There is island music we dance to, exotic foods to sample and many shops for the tourist.

We go scuba diving and see the great reef and coral and other sea life. We are having a wonderful time. When we get back to reality of life, and leave paradise, we have to find our first home, but will rent a month to month lease until we find what we are looking for. Everything worked out and we had an apartment already awaiting us upon our return. Kara's parents wanted to give us a gift so they paid rent for three months and had the apartment ready for us as their gift. They were waiting when we returned and had a welcome home party for us. We were settled in our love nest for about four months and found the perfect home. It was a farm house on a private parcel of land. We both fell in love with it as soon as we went to see it. It would be ready in sixty days and we would go to settlement the week before. Kara seemed to be on top of the world, but I noticed at breakfast the smell of food would make her nauseated. We were thinking she could be pregnant, and we were right the test and the doctor's appointment confirmed it. We are having a baby. The baby's due date would be in the summer. Kara loved children and children loved her. She became radiant as this life was forming inside her. I would feel my child move and leap inside Kara. The baby would kick me in the back while I was sleeping. What! a miracle of life. We went to the appointment to see the sonogram and find out the baby's sex. We are having a girl. Kara and I cried at the news of our first child, a daughter. We shopped together and planned every thing for our daughter. The blessed event came, Kara's water had broken at 3:oo a.m. and we had rehearsed what we would do when the time came, we had the suitcase packed and by the door, we had our video camera ready, and we called the hospital before we left. We got to the hospital, went to sign Kara in and they came and took her in a wheel chair to be examined, and she was dilated seven centimeters. The nurse took her to a room and hooked her up to the fetal monitor and I held her hand and stayed with her, she was ready to give birth and was taken to labor and delivery. In a matter of time our daughter was brought into the world. The nurse put her on her mom's belly and her first cries echoed in my heart. Danielle was born, as her tiny hands reached for mine. I could hardly believe the excitement that fills your heart at the moment a life is created. We held our daughter and bonded as a family. My parents came in and saw their first grandchild, and Kara's came in also and held her and loved her. Kara and Danielle would be coming home the next day. We took video of mommy's first day home, and took lots of pictures of our little girl. The next few weeks our parenting skills were being tested and tried, and we both had a new boss in the house. The news flashed a draft would be coming soon, and more of our serviceman and women would be going to Iraq. My heart sank when the day came that our platoon would be going on a tour of duty. Time seemed to stand still. I would brave this and return home to my new daughter and wife. I held onto the thought that this would be short term. I had to stay another term and have been there two years. The way life is dealt, you never know what is going to happen. I braved the enemy fire and got hit with the shard of a bullet in my left leg; I went into get another soldier out of danger and was given a purple heart for my bravery. I am going home today and will be with my wife and daughter, and I will never take for granted the frailty of life and how quickly one can loose it.

Psalm 28:7 The Lord is my strength and my shield; my heart trusteth in Him, and I am helped; therefore my heart greatly rejoiceth; and with my song will I praise Him.

Enemy Lines

The Calm Before The Storm

This is the heartbreaking story of the war through a soldier's eyes. You are trained to know who you're enemy is, there are many weapons you get to experiment with. You're rifle and militant armory is you're best friend. You see children crying in the streets. People begging for a morsel of food. You see people blown to bits right before you're very eyes. You see blood shed and know the purpose. There are car bombings, explosives, explosives strapped to children. There is the enemy watching you, he knows your whereabouts, when you lie down to sleep. You sleep with one eye open. The buddy system is in effect, you're buddy is your eyes and you're ears. You are trained to kill. You cannot think about your past life at home, how much you miss you're families. If you're mind wanders too far, you will be unaware of a stranger who would like nothing more than to kill you. When the holidays come and you think how much you miss you're holiday traditions, you are just thankful to be alive one more year to celebrate with your brothers and sisters in the service. You think about your wife, or girlfriend, or fiancée, how much you would love to be there to enjoy the life you left behind for the cause of the price of freedom. You think of your parents who raised you to become the man you've become. The birthday parties, graduation party's, family gatherings, and stages of life that you once had. Receiving letters of a home you once occupied, life events that are happening while you are away. The elements of weather you have to battle. Sleeping quarters can sometimes be a trench of dirt. The grueling, aching body that is sleep deprived, but always alert, looking over you're shoulder. When a building is collapsed from enemy fire, you see the body's brought out and heaped up, to sort out later. The phone calls home to announce a son, or daughter, or other is deceased. Mother's praying for the safety of their children, giving them to the Lord for His protection in their lives. The nameless soldiers who are recognized on a wall of remembrance. Wondering if you are ever going to see another sunset. The casualties of war ponder you're thoughts. As the enemy draws closer, who will be quicker to act on the moment? You know that these armies of soldier's wish to extinguish you're life. You wonder how someone can hate you so much. They are programmed to hate you and are told that you're the enemy. The dictator's rule their lives. The dictator's will have them killed if they don't comply with their way of living. You see a fearful people who will die with suicide bombings, to prove a point. These people think it is gain to die, a victory in a sense. You see and hear of cars and buses being bombed. Planes go down in flames. The stench of death is in every corridor. People walk into sniper areas and die a painful death. The wounded are taken to the hospitals, but are never the same after seeing the faces of death on a daily basis. It becomes a way of life. What you wouldn't give to be back on American soil, in the safety zone.

You dream of the day you will feel the ground beneath you're feet, back in the good ole USA, you get off the plane and kiss the ground. You never take for granted home sweet home; you're children's smiles, a neighbor's need, a kind word or a forgiving heart. The grip of reality that you will see another sun set, take another moonlit walk, smell the flowers along the way, embrace you're loved ones. Embrace each day with a positive attitude; I can make a difference in my life, and in the lives of others. To walk down the street, without the fear of being ambushed and tortured or a POW (prisoner of war). This is a very realization of what can happen in a war torn country. Being able to lie down and sleep without the fear of enemy fire. Having all you're medical needs met when a problem arises. The right kind of medicine, clean, sterile equipment used to address the medical issues. Proper nutrition to fuel the body's health. Watching your baby take his or her first steps. Praying with your children. Being there to hear their first cries as they are brought into the world. Being there to cut the cord and witness the miracle of birth. Taking classes at a local college to further your education. Helping your children learn their ABC's, going on field trips, seeing your daughter at her first prom, walking your daughter down the aisle on her wedding day. You're son's first little league game, catching that fly ball, getting his first home run, learning to drive. Celebrating holidays with the one's you love, picking out the tree, bringing the tree home, setting the tree up, decorating with the lovely lights, candles in the window, wreath on the front door. Watching the snow fall, tasting snow cream, opening your presents while the camera is in motion. Spending time with your grandparents, listening to the way of life they have had to endure. Going to a movie and dinner with your wife. Holding and caressing your wife as you are one. Sitting together by a warm fire as you chase the chills away. Reminiscing about days gone by, your first romantic stare and later your first kiss. Your first date, when you couldn't wait to see her. You're rehearsed proposal and praying she will say yes. On bended knee, pledging you're everlasting love, the ring that you worked overtime to pay for. Your plans to get married, the wedding date, guests, wedding party, rehearsal, rehearsal dinner, invitations, etc. Honey moon plans, destination, and how long you will be gone. Where you will live, future plans, etc. Learning the things you love and dislike about each other. The toothpaste in the sink, the toilet seat up, socks on the floor, a clean house, take out, or her cooking, clean shirts, lawns mowed. The little perks we learn about each other. We learn how to share the same room in the house; we learn what consumed time is about, late schedules, bills to be paid, anniversary dinners and forgotten anniversaries. How to entertain guests when they pop in unexpected. Having an extra gift when someone arrives late. The new in-laws and out-laws that put in their two sense worth. Sleeping in late occasionally to catch up on a good night's sleep. A job promotion that comes right on time. Getting back to the real world to the things that matter the most, like the unconditional love of your family, who is your heart beat and strength in the heat of the battle. It is very rewarding to fight for our country, and the patriotism that stirs within my soul, however I love my homeland and wish to stay on non-enemy ground to establish my life's purpose with the one's I love.

Psalm 144:1 Blessed be my Lord my strength, which teacheth my hands to war, and my fingers to fight.

A Quest for Peace

Ever since the beginning of war, we have wanted a cease-fire peace offering. Why can't countries just get along? Why does there have to be blood shed?

Iraq and Iran have always been allies. Where is the common ground? Why do the people of the third world countries think they own land that is divided? There are always casualties of astronomical numbers of those killed in action, POWS, the soldiers on the front line, and others who can't be identified except through dental x-rays. This is the way it has always gotten done, since the beginning of time. Israel is one of the most war torn countries, because Palestinian would like to drive them into the sea. Iran and Iraq have always wanted to reclaim "their land" There is an American interest in Israel, first and foremost the holocaust committed by Hitler. The holocaust was a very horrific picture of what can happen when a dictator has a rise to power and the Jewish people were at his mercy. He had trained armies to try to kill everyone of Jewish decent. The world watched in horror as the scene of unthinkable human cruelty was portrayed at the hand of a madman. The people who were taken to the concentration camps only to be martyrs. The starvation pictures that we have seen on the media make anorexia look like a walk in the park. This was a very demon possessed man whose father was satan. He was a world leader, who wanted to totally rid the world of Jewish people. The Torah, the first five books of the bible quotes, "I will bless those who bless you, and I will curse those who curse you." The fear of the Lord is the beginning of wisdom. Israel is Gods chosen people. The land of Israel belongs to the Jewish people. Israel has won wars against such powerful enemies and insurmountable odds, because God has been there with them in the battle. If America doesn't stand by and support Israel, the blessings and prosperity of our nation will be removed. Israel is a democracy. Israel is an asset to the United States; they would offer an olive branch to promote peace in the Middle East. A key American interest is the Saudi monarchy, because it assures the flow of oil at reasonable prices. Iraq also has oil fields and other exports to the U.S. As terrorism has struck our American soil, Israel has always faced terrorism and have won victorious. Israel shed no tears over Saddam's demise, and it gave full support to the United States once the Bush Administration made its choice. When Saddam invaded Kuwait he declared that" he would make fire eat up half of Israel if Israel tries to do anything against Iraq." This threat was meant to win him Arab-Muslim support, but his real objective was to protect the oil-soaked Gulf. When he threatened Israel, he attacked weaker allies, Kuwait. Quite simply, from a realist point of view, Israel has been a low-cost way of keeping order in the Middle East, managed off-shore by the United States and without the commitment of any force. The United States brought Israel entirely into its orbit making of it a dependent client through arms and aid. Due to American support for Israel, the corner of the Middle East along the eastern Mediterranean has been free of crises requiring direct American military intervention. This is due to American support for Israel. Continue to pray for Israel, for they are a key to future events to Jesus return.

Speaking of the situation in the Persian Gulf, where American allies are weak. There a terror sponsoring regime is still bent on driving out American forces out of the gulf. United States was once deemed a "pillar has collapsed in the face of an anti-American upsurge, producing the humiliation of a hostile regime. Saddam launched an eight year bloody war against Iran that ushered in terrorism, and produced waves of anti-American terror, by occupying Kuwait and threatening Saudi Arabia. The other cell terror groups that still remain a threat are: Hezbollah, al –Queda are just a few in operation. Hezbollah is trying to make Israel look like they are at fault for the war crimes in Lebanon. This terrorist group committed war crimes in the recent war that far exceed in quantity and gravity for all that Israel is accused of. In the civilian areas of northern Israel, far away from plausible military targets, Hezbollah launched thousands of rocket and mortar attacks. They used protected persons as human shields in the residential areas, hospitals and schools. Hezbollah builds its headquarters in densely populated areas, embeds its fighters in villages and towns, and deliberately places missiles in private homes, even constructing additions to existing structures. They endanger their own citizens, but run the risk of killing innocent people and invite diplomatic pressure to stand down. al Queda has been another force of evil in our not so perfect world. al Queda has committed crimes against humanity for the purpose of their lead man Saddam, and I am sure Ben Laden. What is Ben Laden? Houdini? He can stay one step ahead of the manhunt? He needs to be brought to justice also. I thought this was an interesting quote by Henry Davis Thoreau- There are a thousand hacking at the branches of evil to one who is striking at the root. There have been many persons through out history who have been in a leadership position, and have used evil to commit hideous crimes of humanity, but in the end they are brought down." Sin is only for a season." "Your sin will find you out." There is a day of reckoning; everything in the dark will be brought out in light. The Shiite death squads are in full force, going into crowded market places and blending in only to rein terror on the unsuspecting innocent lives. The media is only able to capture so much of this. These types of crimes are happening more frequently in the streets of Baghdad. The innocent are wearing a bull's eye on their backs and are the target for this type of terrorism.

America please pray for peace on earth, good will toward men. Peace will come upon this earth when Jesus rules and reigns with a rod of iron. Continue to pray for Israel for they are the apple of His eye.

Psalm 71:2 Deliver me in thy righteousness, and cause me to escape: incline thine ear unto me, and save me.

Tranquility

Peace In The Midst Of A Storm

The word tranquility represents calmness; peacefulness; quiet; serenity, a disposition free from stress or emotion. Doesn't that sound like music to your ears? If only we could have a life free from stress, we wouldn't have a need for anti-depressants and other garden variety of stress relievers. Sounds like a perfect world to me. The Middle East is on the brink of a civil war. You see the media daily reminding us of what we already know. How much more to we have to endure? When will it ever end? Israel has always been the center of catastrophe. Hitler wanted to wipe them out as you learned in the earlier chapters. The Jewish people were given the Promised Land. Israel is the land of opportunity. Just a quick reflection of what took place on September 11-2001, as we all know, the terrorist were busy planning the attack on The World Trade Center, Pentagon, and the planes that were hijacked as an off course plot unfolded. We watched as the media captured the unimaginable. People were at work and were planning their day only to be caught up in the aftermath of explosion, death, and emergency 911. People were running and searching for their loved ones, the children in the day care centers, the fathers and mother's and sisters and brothers, after the smoke wore off, pictures were carried with the survivors in hope of uncovering their loved ones with an expression of hopefulness that maybe they were alive, a glimmer of hope shadowed their minds. The random act of immeasurable violence had taken the lives of so many. There were a few people who for whatever reason stayed home that day, or called in sick. God knew this was going to happen, He wasn't caught off guard, He didn't wink at the evil, the people who were left, held hands with a stranger, and cried and bowed in prayer for the victims, and victim's families'. America was shaken, the safe world that we had know changed forever. The new world order was now at hand. The Homeland Security had come into play. The Security Alert System was put into place to measure the threat risks, and a hotline was set up to call in if you see a suspicious act. We needed to protect our waterways as well as our homeland which was now in jeopardy. The airports also heightened security. The arrival time to be at the airport was lengthened so as to check out everything. Our lives were changed and altered forever. We cannot allow terrorist to threaten our future and our children's future. There were a lot of unseen heroes, who were behind the scenes of the catastrophe, cleaning up and helping to restore what had been destroyed. Thank you to the fireman, and police men, and hospital personnel, and people who left their families to be a very present help to the people in New York City. Bravo! to those who gave their time, energy and love to the wounded. To all the people who sent money, supplies, food, etc. May God bless your families. Gods word says if you've done this unto the lest of my brethren you've done it unto me. When we give of ourselves, we are a reflection of Gods love to other people.

In Gods timetable of events to come, there will be peace in the midst of a storm.

When the time of Jacob's trouble comes as the bible has foretold, the last days will be upon the earth. People will live as in the days of Noah, they were eating, and drinking, and marrying and the flood came and the door was shut, and eight souls were saved. The whole world was washed away, all the evil that was done, had come to a bitter end. God put a rainbow in the sky as a symbol as to never cover the entire world with water again. God cannot change, He is the same yesterday, today, and forever, and His word is the truth, and what His word says, mark it down it will come to pass. Prophecy is being fulfilled everyday as the last days are quickly approaching. When the curtain closes and the tribulation period is ushered in, there will be three and a half years of peace, and people will think that the son of perdition is the real Messiah, he will rule and reign from his father's throne, he will do miracles and signs and wonders. Many people will be deceived. In the midst of the tribulation all hell will break loose, and the wrath of God will be poured out upon mankind. In Revelation, the last book of the bible, it is very clear what will happen. The seals are opened and there are four horsemen, the first being a white horse who went forth conquering and to conquer. The second seal was opened and a red horseman was given power to take peace from the earth. The third horse was black, and that horseman was given balance in each hand. The fourth was opened and that horseman was pale and his name that sat on him was death. The fifth seal was opened and the souls of those who had been slain for the word of God, and for the testimony they held; The sixth seal was opened and there was a great earthquake; and the sun became black as sack cloth of hair, and the moon became as blood; and the stars of Heaven fell unto the earth; and the heaven departed as the scroll; and every mountain and island were moved out of their places; Kings and great men and other men hid themselves in the dens and the rocks of the mountains; and said to the mountains and rocks to Fall on us and hide us from the face of Him that sitteth upon the throne, and from the wrath of the lamb. The seventh seal was opened and seven angels were given seven trumpets, each angel is commanded to sound the trumpet and carry out what God has told them to do.) Revelation 6-8) when you read the bible and understand what is coming up, it can help you to understand who the winner is. Jesus Christ. When Jesus returns He will return to the Mount of Olives. The Jews who have been spiritually blinded will one day know their Messiah and receive Him. The events in the Middle East are happening to usher in the second coming of Christ. (King James Version).

II Thessalonians 2:8 And then shall that Wicked be revealed, whom the Lord shall consume with the spirit of His mouth, and shall destroy with the brightness of His coming.

Letters Home & Quotes from the Homeland

The letters that I am going to share with you are from the ministry to Support our Soldiers/ Tiny Hands, an organization founded by Gracie Brown, and her husband, Paul in 2004. Gracie known as "nana" started sending boxes of supplies to the soldiers who were in the most need; another part of this was the beginning of Tiny Hands, an organization to send supplies for the children in orphanages. Rita then expanded the ministry for the soldiers to give gifts to the Iraqi children, and through the military police, the children would gain trust with the soldiers. Donations are sent to Gracie and Paul Brown, and Rita and Terry Farmer, and are sent to the foreign lands where they are much needed. Rita who is Gracie's daughter, along with her husband, Terry have partnered with Gracie to help with this much needed ministry. Donations are accepted as well as the surmountable amount of money needed for postage. If you would like to help in any way please call 1-(410)-658-2987.

Donations Needed: Letters to the Soldiers (They need to hear from you)

Soccer balls, hand-held electronic games, hygiene items, phone cards (AT&T)

All-occasion cards, school supplies (pencils, sharpeners, note pads), frebreeze,candles.

Clothing for men and women: boot socks (black, tan, olive green)

Crew socks white all sizes

Boxers

Tee-Shirts Tan or sand colored (all sizes)

Rice and dried beans (larger size)

Prohibited items (cannot send) glass, aerosol cans, inappropriate pictures or reading material.

Thank you in advance for your support. May God bless you and send blessings unto you for giving a small part back to the soldiers who are in the battle-zone fighting for your freedom, and keeping terrorist out of our country.

My name is JD and I am with the 385th Military Police Battalion from Fort Steward, Georgia. One of your Any Soldier packages happened to reach our destination in Afghanistan. I just wanted to take a few moments to thank you and tell you a little bit about all of us here. We left Fort Steward in November of this year, so we have only just begun our tour of duty here. Some of us have served overseas before in either Iraq or Afghanistan. However, many have not. It is such a great thing to know that there are people back home that still support what we do. With all of the controversy in the news about the War on Terror, it sometimes seems that people in the U.S. are loosing faith. But, then we get care packages and letters from people like you. Thank you so much again for thinking of us, and taking the time to show us that you care.

Sincerely, JD

3RD STRYKER BRIGADE COMBAT TEAM 2ND INFANTRY DIVISION

We would like to thank you very much for your support. An everyday American having communication with troops from the frontlines of war really helps to boost our morale.

War is an ugly thing, but as Aristotle said, "We make war that we may live in peace." It is our hope that this war will not be fought for much longer, but never will we forget the sacrifices our fallen and wounded comrades have made whether in this war or previous.

Thank you for keeping us in your thoughts.

Delta 1st Platoon

We all want to thank you for the things that you have sent. We also want to thank you for taking time out of your busy life to pray for us and send us things. We thank you from the bottom of our hearts. Even though we are away from our family's it is like you that you help us get through the days. Once again we thank you.

Thank you,
Delta 1st Platoon

RE: Thank You

Thank you for your kind note. Speaking to you earlier today was a great blessing to me, though your tears made my heart skip a beat or two! I am so thankful that God put your ministry on my heart. I realized that I could have easily excused the advertisement on 103.7, but it wasn't until the 3rd time to hear that I had a pen to take down the phone number. Praise God- we are both blessed.

Thank you again for your commitment to the ministry God has placed on your heart. May our troops and the little ones overseas be blessed and may the Good News of Jesus Christ be spread. In His grip, NG

HUGS AND KISSES FROM KUWAIT

They sometimes put their own spin on things in the news but then there is also a lot that they don't know about and leave out especially a lot of things that go on in the outside fire bases, like the one I am at, but here it has been a lot that has been going on this week and last week alone that will really make you open your eyes and really pay attention. Like within one day last week, we took 30 rockets at our camp, they really had me and my guys pinned down, so we couldn't get to our cannon to fire back at them, cause every time that we went to lie on the target the rockets would continue to come at us till I told the guys that sends the missions down to use it to the other gun so I can get into the fight and then still as they were coming in I kept all my guys in the bunker and I ran out and stayed out there to set all the information on the gun, still pausing to lay on the ground, when the next rocket was coming in, but then I jumped back up to finish what I was doing, and then when I finally got laid on the target, that is when I called my guys out, so we could finally fire back at them. And now everyday since we take 8-10 rockets a day following the same routine, because they really know where my gun is and they're aiming for it to take it out to collect the 200,000 reward for destroying a cannon or a 2,000 bounty on my sections head. I do what I do for my kids and all the other kids so that they will be able to live in the land of the free and hopefully not have to worry about going to war and doing any of this.

We are following orders that are sent down from the President. Sent on our tour of duty away from our families so the war doesn't come to our country, like what started with 9/11.

Thank you from Afghanistan

God bless you! Thank you for your support. You obviously realize that it is by helping us to help the children here that we will ultimately help those folks make their country safe and democratic (in their own model), and get us out of here (except maybe to visit as tourists). Woe be to all of us if any of our kids and grandkids should ever have to come over here in a role similar to one that myself and the others here are on for 16 months of irreplaceable time in our lives. I am truly touched by your story, and am greatly inspired that you take time to send us so much wonderful stuff.

Only when they know the four universal freedoms (freedom to worship as they see fit, freedom of expression, freedom from want, and the freedom from fear) will the world be a better place, and will we in our wonderful country be truly safe. We have a saying here, "happy people don't join the Taliban or Al Queda."

It is because of outstanding Americans like you all that we are winning here, and we ARE winning here.

Love, SG

Major, Engineers, US Army

The 62nd Engineer Combat Battalion

As I sit down to write this final note home I have began to think about the events of the past year and breathe a huge sigh of relief that we (the 62nd Engineer Combat Battalion) are 2 weeks away from flying back to FT. Hood, Texas.

This past year has been a combination of many things to include: (too many to count), accounting for 780 Soldiers in various locations throughout Iraq, multiple

Finance transactions to ensure every Soldier received their deployment entitlements, awards (over 2100 of various types), promotion ceremonies for enlisted personnel and 15 officers, multiple award ceremonies for enlisted personnel as well as junior officers promoting over 230 enlisted personnel and 15 officers, multiple award ceremonies, and many long days spent at a desk processing paperwork. Seems as though I take the time to clean out the paperwork in my inbox everyday but I never have quite enough time to send a quick note home to those who mean the most to me. So this note is to say Hi, and to let you know that the "I am thinking of you" is long overdue, but I wanted to take the time to let you know that I appreciate your support that you have given to me and all the personnel serving in the Armed Forces! Without dedicated support from our loved ones back home our year would have been difficult.

Camp Liberty is bursting at the seams with Soldiers; multiple units are in the process of transitioning their battle space so there are about double the number of Soldiers living on the camp. Our replacement unit has arrived and our transition of battle space has begun as well. As we turn over the office of the 20th Engineer Battalion we continue to wrap up the never ending "last minute" award, report or memorandum to process. I appreciate your dedicated support through thoughts, prayers, letters, and care packages over this past year! As I near the end of the deployment and prepare to travel home< I would like you to know that your kindness and generosity will not be forgotten. As for future plans, my family still thinks I am going to stay for active duty… (two years ago I said I was going to get out of the Army and changed my mind… hence how I ended up in Iraq for the second time), but I am really getting out this time! My paperwork has been submitted, and I am patiently waiting to receive my orders to get out. If all goes as planned I will be heading home March 2007. I plan on spending quality time with my family and friends, many of whom I have not seen very much over the past four years, and I am going to relax and enjoy life as a civilian again ha-ha.

I look forward to 2007 and everything it has in store! I am thankful for the great friends I have made while in the Army as well as my experiences and travel opportunities.

Thank you again for your continued support! Wishing you a safe and happy holiday season and a blessed New Year!

"Freedom isn't free, just ask my son." "God bless our troops, guide them and protect them, hide them in the cleft of thy rock." "God bless our fallen heroes."

"To my grandsons, JM, GS & SW with love from your nanny, I am proud of you."

Praying fervently for you, from Restoration Family Worship Center in Peach Bottom, Pa. Praying, from Center Grove Baptist Church. DFM. (Georgia)

Matthew 25:40 And the King shall answer and say unto them, Verily, I say unto you, Inasmuch as ye have done it to one of the least of my brethren, ye have done it unto me.

Fighting for Freedom

The Heroic Story Of Rn Cl

From the time I was in elementary school, where I grew up in Boston, Massachusetts, I knew my calling in this life would be to help people who were hurting, I rescued kittens in our neighborhood and would nurse them back to health, using bandages to cover where their hair once was, and an eye dropper to feed them with,(if they were too young to eat on their own.) My friends would call and ask me to check out their pets as well. I became the nurse mate of our street. My parents supported my need to help the helpless and for my seventh birthday I got a doctor's kit, my mom made a white jacket and embroidered my name on it. I felt very good that I would one day wear a white uniform as a nurse and eagerly set out my course to future goal setting. Through my middle school years I had health class and paid much attention to my teacher. It was here that valuable life lessons were taught. When I turned sixteen I applied for a candy striper in our local general hospital and during the summer I met a lot of nice people who helped to pave the way to a medical profession. I would visit my floor of patients assigned and also be on call to visit another candy striper's patients. I found myself listening to the elderly as they had a desperate cry for help for the loneliness of missed visits from family's who were to involved in their own lives to pay a simple visit. A little history of my family is, I have one older brother Jason, who does what most big brothers do, protect his baby sister. My mom has climbed the corporate ladder since before I was born, she is CEO of a major Corporation for aerospace materials. My father's job is a prestigious one as well; he is a scientist, for a major chemical corporation. My parents have always inbred in us to set our goals to attain excellence in what ever field we choose. The summer before my graduation, I called a family meeting, I wanted to discuss joining the US Air Force, everyone was happy for me. My senior year, I only needed three credits to finish school, so I had to go to school a half a day.

When I came home at noon I started going to the library and studying medical terminology and psychology 101. Many days were spent huddling over a stack of books. I was like a sponge and couldn't get enough knowledge. The spring was coming up quickly as I was preparing for graduation. My senior pictures went over without a hitch. I took a Saturday to talk to an Air Force recruitment officer about their scholarship program for nursing. I could join as soon as summer or fall. Wow! was I excited. Most of my friends would be planning their lives for the summer after senior week; I wanted to get ready for boot camp. So after a fun filled week of senior blitz, baking on the beach, eating junk food out, and hanging out with my friends, who I am happy to say are straight, we said our good byes and hugged as if we wouldn't see each other for some time. I got an official letter from my recruitment officer for my departure for boot camp. My destination would be San Antonio, Texas. In two days I would go to the main processing building and be sworn in, to serve our country. My parents and brother and best friend,

Gina would accompany my last day to the airport. As we awaited my flight plans, we reminisced about our good times and bad times and had a few laughs. We hugged and said our good byes as I boarded my plane. My dad waved a kiss as he did when I was a child. My mom's eyes filled with tears, gave a look of "I miss you already. " I boarded the plane and took my assigned seat. It was an extremely long flight, I wrestled with the idea of trying to sleep, but was too excited to start my new journey. I looked out the passenger window to the tiny objects below, the cars looked like match box toys. I was nearer to heaven I thought, I prayed for the safety of the flight and did some much needed soul searching. Many hours later we landed safely as a bus awaited our arrival and drove us to San Antonio, where we were greeted by our sergeant. We were given our bunks, our gear, etc. It was late so we bunked down for the night.

The next day we lined up for breakfast, did several laps around the track, went into the medical building, got our shots, guys got haircuts; we got our days assignments and our fatigues. The next morning at 4 am, I awoke to the sound of loud bells and yelling of my fellow soldiers. Our sergeant was ready to show us the ropes. We had marching duty; we marched around the base five times. After lunch we went through an obstacle course of running through the tires and jumping and leaping, and climbing ropes. The next few hours we were crawling through some pretty tight spaces, and learning how to throw a grenade, we were taught about how to clean our guns and ammunitions. I never knew there was so much to learn during basic training, better known as "boot camp". Another part of becoming a well trained soldier is learning about the chemical warfare and wearing the appropriate gear of respirators, and suiting up. We had some drills in which a smoke screen was used during these exercises, and we had only seconds to get to safety. The time goes pretty quickly when your days are jam packed and exhaustion becomes a way of life. Graduation is nearing and there is a ceremony held in honor of you passing basic training. "Congratulations! everyone passed. Stage two, your assignment to your new destination. My orders say I am staying in Texas. The next day we will be boarding buses, planes etc. I will be starting my nursing classes at a local college at night and staying on our base during the day. I gather my books and head off to further my career. While at lunch I meet some new acquaintances, and we meet up everyday for lunch, a friend sets up a blind date without my knowing. He walks over to the table, introduces himself and joins us for lunch. My friends all of a sudden have a hidden agenda and we are setting alone. I introduce myself and we share some time over a hamburger and milk shake. I find out Brent is also on base, he is here for the duration, just as I am. We exchange information and decide to see one another again. Next time we meet he tells me about his future goals in the service. He wants to work for the Pentagon, just as his grandfather and father have done. He wants to be in the secret service. I think that is to be admired when a man knows what he wants to do. The next several months we continue to date and become much closer. We both have leave in six months for Christmas. When the time comes to join our families for the holidays, Brent tells me he would like to visit my hometown. We fly to Boston, Massachusetts and rent a car and surprise my parents. The plane lands and the snow is falling, we make it to my parents on time for the carving of the turkey. We pull up to the driveway, anticipation of seeing my family consumes my rapidly beating heart. I tell Brent to dodge out of sight so I can have my parents be surprised. I walk up and ring the doorbell, my father smiles as he sees me, the tears streaming down his face.

When he opens the door we embrace and mom comes running. We huddle together then I introduce Brent to them. Jason is down stairs and comes upstairs to see what all the noise is about. I hug my brother and we go inside and sit at the dining room table and have prayer before we eat. My dad asks for the blessing as we begin to talk and reminisce. The house is decorated as it is everywhere you look. Mom and I retreat to the kitchen and dad, Brent and Jason to the living room. Brent will be grilled about daddy's little girl, I have prepared him in advance. He passes the test with flying colors. Mom and I go out to do last minute shopping. Brent and dad and Jason stay behind at the house. When we get back home, Brent takes the rental car with Jason and does a little shopping of his own. The next morning we have breakfast together and start our traditional Christmas morning. Breakfast, then opening of the gifts. Each person is given a gift and we open them in unisom. Brent hands a small box decorated with a big red ribbon to me and gets down on one knee and proposes in the company of my brother and parents.

The ring is a brilliant emerald cut carat with ruby stones set on the sides of it. It is absolutely stunning! "Yes I will be your wife," was my reply through the tears. That was a total surprise. My parents and brother were overjoyed. We discussed having a small traditional wedding or to elope. My family said they would join us, and we planned to elope to St. Thomas, my mom and dad as witnesses. We got our flight plans for the following week. From the airport we boarded a cruise ship, set to take us to our wedding destination. Mom gave me her wedding gown and we were set to say our nuptials. In a very secluded remote spot on the island we exchanged our wedding vowels and became Mr. & Mrs. Brent Collins. Our parents said goodbyes, and we retreated to our island paradise to dance the night away and enjoy island food, fun and our awaited honeymoon. After seven days of marital bliss, we board our plane and arrive back at my parent's house. In two weeks we are due back in Texas. We spend time seeing the sights of Boston, and visiting friends and family. We take one week to fly to Maine to meet Brent's parents and family. I am welcomed with open arms. Brent's mom and dad are happy to see us and I meet Brent's siblings, Amanda 12, and Eric 16. What a wonderful family unit. I see where Brent gets his good looks from his dad. And Brent's mom's sweet kind disposition is a wonderful trait to inherit from your mother. He has the best of both of them in him. We get ready in a few days to return to our lives in Texas. When we get back to Texas the war has already begun, and some of our fellow soldiers have been deployed to Iraq and Afghanistan and Kuwait. Several months pass and both of us have our deployment date for Baghdad; Brent leaves one week before me. We have prayed together for our safe return. Brent gets there and is settled in his mission, I am called into action. We have fire drills and missions training. guns are firing in the background. There are POW'S who have been ambushed and captured. We have seen Iraqi television, televising their unnatural demands for the release of these people. "Oh God I pray let a miracle happen for these people." The next several days we are briefed on search and seize rescue. I will wear my nurse's uniform and go in to the place the POW'S are being held and will escort a POW (giJane Doe) to the nearest exit and take her to the station for first aid, there an ambulance will be waiting, and then the squad can be cleared to surround the building and get the POW'S out. This is an extremely high tech operation, anything can go wrong. We plan our mission, mission complete. POW'S are taken to safety and I am awarded for my bravery. During the ceremony I am given a congressional medal of honor. My husband is very proud of me and salutes my courageous spirit. We both have planned when our time is over here, we will not reenlist but plan our future together. We have put in our orders to go home, it is granted. We decide to live in Washington, DC where Brent gets a job as a secret service agent in the Pentagon. I am pregnant expecting our first child. I will work as a RN in a general hospital until I have to take off for maternity leave. Our baby is due in the spring. Brent goes to each visit with me to the obstetrician; today we will learn we are having a daughter.

We are very excited and overwhelmed how life happens. We were once thousands of miles away from the wiles of this common world. We were fighting for your freedom, cannons firing, guns firing, enemy fire and death all around us.

Not sure if we would ever return to our family's and granted ways of life. Now look at us, we are going to be first time parents with a vision to be the best we can be. We want freedom for our children and future generations. We have bought our first house and have come along way from the trenches of time through the wiles of the war to be here. God has a planned purpose for our lives He has a "blueprint" our DNA of what He would have us to become for His purpose. The flowers are blooming and a new life has arrived, at 3:00 am on April 28th-2006, Brittany Danielle Collins has entered the world. She weighs in at 7lbs.7 oz. She has a full head of dark hair and blue eyes, just as her daddy does.

We look upon life's greatest miracle counting her tiny hands and toes, a perfect little lamb, a gift from God. Our family circle is now complete. She has her dad's set of lungs as her first cries are heard. Our family's hear the blessed news and huddle with us admiring and giving thanks for our little miracle. Grandparents hold and cuddle their first grandchild. Pictures are taken as this little girl has brought so much joy. In a day or two we will be coming home. Brent video's Brittany's welcome home. The house is decorated with pink and yellow ribbon, balloons, and party favors. Family and friends gather around to offer congratulations. We hold hands and pray for Gods blessing on our little girls life.

We will continue to be in Gods will for our lives, we pray for our fellow brothers and sisters who are still on enemy ground, amidst the controversial war times.

Praying God will bring them safely through as He is our refuge in times of trouble.

Mark 14:38 Watch ye and pray, lest ye enter into temptation. The spirit truly is ready, but the flesh is weak.

Missing You

Memoirs Of A Life Time Of Love (Db)

I am an only child, and my life has always been exciting. The spoiled little daddy's girl and mommy's girl bring back some very good memories. There was no competition, so my mom and dad gave in to my every whim. We live in the big city of life in the fast lane. The big apple, New York City. I love city life and couldn't begin to imagine life in the country or any other place. My summers were spent going to nice vacation spots on Long Island and traveling, camping, and hanging out with my friends. Friends were almost always invited to go with us so I could enjoy activities with them. I always wondered what it would be like to have siblings, I would dream about it but it never happened so it became a fleeting thought. Through my school years I aced at academic performance. I was in our middle school band and played clarinet. I also got into sports. I was on the swim team, and also played soccer. My mom was mom's taxi, but she didn't complain because she was a part of what I loved to do. On Tuesday night the parents would meet after practice or a game and we would have potluck dinner or go to a local restaurant, those were the best and closest times. When I entered into high school I continued to excel in my grades, and was preparing to earn a scholarship, I wanted a business degree like my dad, who was a Certified Public Accountant. He would show me a few pointers when I asked him to. My mom stayed at home so she could be there for me. She did get into a business through the internet part time and has done very well as a data entry clerk. "I am so proud of her." Today we will elect our student body president, the ballots are cast and the votes are in. My name is announced as this year's participant. Congratulations! My classmates and faculty congratulate me. My parents are very proud and we go out to my favorite restaurant, Red Lobster. The next day at school the student body meets and plans are made for the upcoming prom, football games, and Sadie Hawk's dance (a girl ask a guy to the dance). We plan to have a person for photography for the yearbook and someone to get those awesome shots at our football games and prom. I sign up for accounting 101, data processing, and math courses to get started in my first two years of high school. There will be many nights of cramming and studying. My friends Jackie, and Christina always want to go to the mall, I am focused on studying. My plans are when I get out of school; I want a college education and want to be a Certified Public Accountant and work for the White House to help to relinquish the national deficit. I have been dating for about six months, and Thomas understands my need for career first. He is so sweet and such a hopeless romantic. He leaves love notes in my locker and at my house. He to, is career minded, he wants to be a chemical engineer and has applied to our local college for his first two years. It is week before Sadie Hawk dance and I send Thomas a note for a date, he will pick me up at six for dinner and then off to the dance. I go shopping with mom for casual clothes for my big night out. The next day at school I sit at the lunch table and Christina and Jackie join me, they to have gotten dates for the dance. We will all go to dinner together and go to the dance. Friday comes quickly and I get ready for the dance, Thomas arrives right on time, he has roses for me. Mom puts them in water and takes pictures of us. We meet up with Jackie and Tim, Christina and John and go to dinner. We sit and talk and order our food. We eat and talk and order dessert, pay our bill and leave. We get to the dance, listen to music, hang out with our friends and dance. It is a very fun night out. Summer is right around the corner, I have gotten a work permit and have applied for Lab Technician at the FDA, I should hear about the job in a few days. My plans are to work and save money for college. The job comes through and I am so excited. The interview went better than expected. The following Monday I am to start. I will work forty hours, dayshift from nine to five. My summer went by pretty quickly. School is coming up in a few weeks. I am in my junior year; I have held an honor roll grade point average of 3.8. I am still working toward a scholarship through my dad's company. A recruiter comes to our school and talks to us about joining the military, he says there are college programs available to pay for college. He has caught my interest. I take the paperwork home and discuss this with mom and dad. There is silence at our dinner table but it is my decision and my parents will support my decision. I am proud to join the US Army. "I will make you both proud." I pray for Gods guidance in all life's decisions. I will enroll in the ROTC program after graduation and I will earn my business degree. I will agree for a four year term to serve my country. Thomas is excited for me and plans on relocating with me as soon as we both know where I will be stationed. It is nearing our senior year, and there is still so much to do. Our parents plan for graduation parties for us. The school year seems to move ever so quickly when you are planning on starting your goals after high school. There are many days and nights with your friends and it feels as if time is swiftly clicking away. "Somebody stop that clock." Time is running out for all the good times spent with friends and loved ones. Each day presents new opportunities for maturity and growth; we are leaving our childish ways behind and pressing onto becoming young lady's and young men. We have to make life decisions and learn from them. We have to make our own mistakes and troubleshoot them. We are responsible for our own lives. High School gets us ready to face the everyday realities that life sometimes throws at us. Some of us will go onto college; others will go into employment, while still others have no immediate direction. I go with Jackie and Christina to pick out our prom gowns. We try on quite a few before we find the perfect one. The one I have chosen is a satin off the shoulder dark blue complete with sequins and a lace bodice. I find matching shoes and a shawl to complete my ensemble. I go home, show mom what I bought, she is beaming with pride. I make an appointment with my hairdresser and to have my nails done. Thomas shops for a tuxedo to match what I am wearing. The night of the prom I go to my appointments and get ready for the prom. My hair is in an upswept style, and my nails are polished to perfection. I walk down the stairs, my parents are waiting to video my night at the prom. The doorbell rings and Thomas is there looking handsome as ever. He has gotten a corsage for me and pins it to my dress. We leave and have dinner at a romantic little spot (a favorite of ours). We arrive at our high school prom. He holds me tight and kisses me on the dance floor. We have a curfew and so the night ends. I am too excited to sleep, mom has waited up for me so, and we have our mother- daughter talk. Thomas and I are talking about our future plans; we have been steady for almost four years. There have been times when I thought we had some ripples in the wave of our love. All couples have disagreements and other trials to work through. We have planned after boot camp and our 4 year term to then get married. The next few weeks we are getting ready to graduate. I have prepared my speech as Valedictorian. "My fellow students, student body, and faculty, I want to wish all of you the best of endeavors in what ever path of life you choose, I pray you will spread your wings to new horizons, and you will find peace in your new journey." The audience applauds, and the graduation commencement gets underway. The names and awards of each pupil are called as each one steps up to the stage to claim their diploma and awards. There is a party at my house as well as Thomas's house. We gather with our friends and family's and have a good time as dad is the grill master. He grills chicken and burgers and hotdogs. We have a DJ for our musical entertainment. I open gifts, and we then get ready for Thomas's graduation party. Thomas's parents have also gone all out to celebrate this day. He has all his family there, friends from school and another cookout. His parents are so very proud of his accomplishments. Thomas's gift was a new truck. His dad tosses him the keys to a new four wheel drive truck. He is quite surprised. We stay for a while and later meet up with friends to see a movie. We go with our senior classmates to Long Island for senior week. We have a lot of fun for a week. There is camping, boating, white water rafting, to name a few. The summer is a time for caring and sharing and spending quality time, but as all good times they must end. In the fall I will be going to 'boot camp." I will be going to Oklahoma for my Army training. Thomas and I get our flight plans and pack to go. We say our goodbyes and head off to Oklahoma. Thomas will live in an apartment while I am at boot camp. We arrive, rent a car and Thomas takes me to the base. We embrace and say goodbye for now. I walk in, unpack, meet with fellow soldiers, get acquainted and meet our sergeant. The next few days we are drilled on how to become soldiers. And so it begins the physical activities from day to day. We are given our guns and ammunition and are briefed about weaponry. I shot the guns and the force knocked me down. We had target practice to destroy the enemy. The sound of the guns echoed in my ears. We learned what to do in an ambush drill. We learned to quickly throw grenades and how to become apart of your environment, whether it be a dirt hill or trench, or tree. We practiced exercises in old dilapidated buildings where the enemy could be hiding. My thoughts were constantly about my one true love, Thomas. I was nearing the end of my training and had gotten a few letters from Thomas and a couple of letters from home. It was wonderful to imagine seeing your family through the words written in the letters. I wanted so much to see Thomas's smile and witty charm, which made my heart skip a beat. To feel his lips press against mine, inviting and lovingly. In less than a week I would be finishing basic training and be back in his arms. The day of our graduation mom and dad and Thomas came. My name was called and I graduated. We went to dinner to celebrate. Thomas asks for my hand in marriage. I would be deployed to Baghdad for a year for my tour of duty. Thomas would wait for me to return as we prayed for God's protection and grace. I arrive in Baghdad, a worn torn country, hostile with our presence there. There are land rovers and tanks stationed in the city and surrounding areas. My job is to order and bring materials for ammunitions and first aid supplies to each station as needed. Each day brings many new challenges." I pray everyday for peace in this country. "I see many wounded soldiers and dress their wounds. We are briefed each day about how the mission is to be carried out, what orders are to be carried out. We hear the horrific screams of the wounded, all too real in this place of death. We hear of a plane going down as it enters enemy territory. Today a bus carrying children was bombed by a terrorist cell. Tomorrow is another day. The children are so afraid of us and we are only trying to help them. We have helped to build a school and a medical center. It is a great feeling to accomplish a positive mission and see the results. I get a letter from Thomas he has finished his first year of college and has taken a job for a chemical company. My tour of duty is extended for another year. "I guess I am needed here." Thomas is okay, but plans to get married as soon as I come home. I have another year to be away from my loved ones and my "heartbeat "Thomas. Well another year passes quickly and I am only days away from boarding a plane to get back to my love. He picks me up at the airport, takes me in his arms and embraces me, and plants a loving kiss on my waiting lips. We are going to move to Washington, DC. We already have picked out a small bungalow in a nice neighborhood. Our wedding plans are quickly made. We will wed in New York on Valentine's Day in the company of our family, and friends. My color schemes will be red dresses for my bridesmaids and Black Tuxedos for the groom and groomsmen. Thomas has held onto my engagement ring, and we will add the second circle of love to it. A circle represents never ending love. The morning of my wedding, mom has made my breakfast, has my wedding gown laid out, has given something borrowed, her mother's pearl necklace. Daddy comes in to see his little girl and have a heart to heart talk. It is getting time to get to the church. Thomas is already there, helping his groomsmen to look their best. My girls and I get ready for the big event. My wedding gown is White sequined, lace and pearls, a four foot train and a veil. The wedding march begins as everyone takes their place. Here comes the bride. I am joined with my husband to be. We say our vows one to another and become one. The reception is at a country club. We dance our first dance together as husband and wife. The bridal party sits down to eat and the other tables are dismissed as well. After cutting the cake, we open our gifts, and head out for our honey moon. "What a beautiful memory of true love." We go to our beach retreat and spend our time as husband and wife. Dinner, dancing, and moonlit walks on the beach. Watching the beautiful sunset together and having breakfast on the balcony. We get back home and I receive a letter to be interviewed for a position in the White House as a Certified Public Accountant, which I am happy to say, I am happily employed. Thomas is also living out his dream as a chemical engineer, we are happy just being us. We often think about our fellow comrades that are in third world countries, and pray for their very lives to be protected and shielded against the fiery darts of the wicked one. I have friends who I still keep in touch with, and continue to pray for. We need to always keep in remembrance the fallen heroes who have taken the bullets and shards of metal in our stead.

Proverbs 12:7 The wicked are overthrown, and are not: but the house of the righteous shall stand.

Homecoming Day

War within the gates (SM's Story) Flight of the Blackhawk

I joined the United States Marine Corps Reserve in June 1983. I had filled out a card a month earlier to get an iron sticker with a bulldog on it; the card was an information card for recruiters. A recruiter called me and started talking about the Marine Corps Reserve as a way to get some help with college expenses. My dad also liked the idea of me joining the Marine Corps, he is a former Marine who served back in the 50's. I left for Paris Island in July 1983.

I have been married for over sixteen years; my wife, Elaine is a schoolteacher. I have three children; Lindsay, my daughter who will be fifteen in April, Austin and Shane are my two sons. They are thirteen and ten respectively.

Boot camp was my first real time away from home. It was quite an experience, one I am glad I went through. I arrived at Paris Island in the dark of the night with a busload of fellow recruits. Before the sun came up we were shaved bald, made to send a formed letter home, letting our families know we had arrived safely and would be busy for the next couple of days, and would write soon.

Several weeks into boot camp our platoon was given our second PT test, our senior drill instructor let it be known that the fastest time in the three-mile run would earn the runner a can of Coke. I went out and run the fastest time in the company. True to his word, my senior drill instructor arrived with my reward. After calling the platoon to attention, I was made to march up and down in front of my platoon singing the Coke a Cola Jingle "it's the real thing", the Coke still tasted great.

The evening before graduating boot camp, I was out on the parade field with the entire company practicing for the next day's graduation. During this time my parents, grandparents and brother showed up. They were told they could go and watch the practice. As they watched the practice, they began looking for me; I was one of the several hundred recruits that were practicing in front of them. In front of the marching platoons were four recruits standing at attention. I was one of these recruits fifteen yards away from my family and they could not find me.

After boot camp I went to Millington Tennessee for training, I spent the winter there before coming home and joining my reserve unit in Willow Grove PA. I had only spent a year away and returned home no worse for the ware, a little heavier and with my one and only tattoo.

I stayed with the Marine Corps reserve until 1987; In October of 1987, I joined the Delaware Army National Guard, with the promise of being sent to flight school, to learn to fly helicopters. In the summer of 1990, I was sent to Fort Rucker, AL, for flight school, I was married three and a half months later. Elaine stayed in our new house in Maryland because of a teaching job. After flight school I returned to the Delaware Army National Guard and flew the UH-1 Huey.

The guard was a good part time job until 2001 after 9-11 things started to change (the guard became much more than a part time job.) In the spring of 2001, I was sent back to Fort Rucker to learn to fly the UH-60 Blackhawk. Then in the spring of 2004, our unit was notified that we would be deploying to Iraq. My first of many painful departures with my family took place. I left again to Fort Rucker, AL in March for a school in Aviation Life Support Equipment (ALSE).

After the completion of ALSE School, I was sent to Fort Dix, NJ where my unit was preparing for Iraq. My unit and I spent a long summer at Fort Dix, we were able to get home most weekends. In October, we had two weeks home for leave, our departure for the desert was set for early November. My second departure took place after my two weeks home. Our departure for the desert was delayed, and we were allowed once again to come home for a couple of days. The early morning of the 9th of November, I again said goodbye. At Fort Dix, on the 10th, we were again delayed and told if we wanted to go home for the night we could, our next planned departure was the 12th. I chose not to go home; I could no longer handle goodbyes with my wife and children. I went to New York visited my sister, visited Ground Zero, and Yankee Stadium.

November 12th, 2005, my unit and I left the United States of America on a plane out of Maguire Air force Base in New Jersey. We arrived in Kuwait, after a long stop in Germany, twenty hours later. My thoughts during the entire flight was wondering how my oldest son's soccer game went. He and his team were playing in an end of the year tournament. They were playing in the finals. (They did win, a fact that I learned several days later).

We spent two weeks in Kuwait before pushing into Iraq. Our one of everything had begun. We all planned on being away for a year and missing one of everything. (Christmas, Birthday's and Anniversaries, etc.).

Iraq was a different world to me, most days were quite routine, the safest place in Iraq is in the air, and we spent a lot of time in the air flying missions. I lived at FOB (Forward Operating Base) Danger at one of Saddam's palace complexes in the heart of Tikrit, on the banks of the Tigris River. Our detachment of three helicopters, six pilots, seven crew chiefs, and two refuels survived a year of daily mortar attacks, occasional gunfire, and several suicide bombers trying to punch holes in the wall of FOB.

With all things going on around us, my biggest problem came in the form of a rodent. When we first arrived, we had quite a rat problem, I had traps sent to me and started to trap them, and my biggest kill was fifteen inches long from head to tail.

We stayed in Iraq until early November 2005, when we left for Kuwait. After two weeks in Kuwait, we loaded on a plane on November 12th, one year to the day after leaving the states. After a long flight home with a couple hours lay over in Ireland, we arrived at Maguire Air force Base in New Jersey. After being bused to Fort Dix, we were given a safety brief and a two-day pass. Our families were waiting in a gym a couple of blocks away. I remember entering the gym and seeing my wife, my children, my parents, and my in-laws. I hugged everyone. The best way I can describe my homecoming, is total joy and relief and a little disbelief that I was home. I remember on the drive home from Fort Dix and just being glad, content. I also was surprised at how much color we have in the northeast. After a year of being in the desert, everything looked so green. Even in the middle of November.

It was great to finally be home, after a two hour drive from Fort Dix. Upon arriving at my house, I noticed it had been decorated with yellow ribbons and a large welcome home sign. The place looked great, and many of my neighbors came out to say hello and greet me. I stood in the street for a couple of minutes and spoke with them, during my time away; they really pitched in and helped my family with plowing snow, lawn work, and our pool.

I finally went into my home, I was finally truly home, a year that seemed so long, some how shortened. I spoke with my family and was surprised by my youngest son with his rendition of Billy Joel's, Piano Man. My youngest son, Shane had just started piano a year before, whenever I spoke with him on the phone, I would ask him how the lessons were going, and if he knew how to play the Piano Man. He would laugh knowing that he was secretly working hard to learn how to play that very difficult song (for an eight year old). When he played it for me it was hard to explain my feelings.

Upon returning to Fort Dix for a week, I spent the next month catching up with my family. My family had changed a great deal, they had become very independent. They did a great job when I was gone, I am very proud of them, especially my wife. They spent a difficult year when I was away, never really knowing what I was doing. My wife and children tackled every problem that arose when I was gone.

Defending Our Homeland (Se's Story)

I was raised in a military family. My father was Active Duty Army. We moved around a lot and got to see so many different things. I believe both my sister and I received a cultural education that you could never teach in school. We lived in the heart of San Francisco, the deep South, and many places overseas. We are a pretty close family, taking pride and admiration in each other. I look at my mother and am in awe that she picked up and moved with two kids and various pets every three or so years. She put her life on pause each time we moved, but she was always there to support my father and the kids. My parents were pretty proud of me joining the Air Force- it was a better choice then the Army when it came to quality of life. My dad immediately purchased a subscription to the Air Force Times for me.

In June 2001, I was commissioned into the United States Air Force. I was finishing up graduate school and was looking for some direction. I didn't want to stay in academia or go on for my PhD. I was thinking about joining the Reserves, so I went to the Recruiting office and started asking around for information. The Air Force recruiter took my name and number and called me a little later and said that the only career field that would fit my education would be Public Health. That sounded great to me. I had to interview with an Active Duty Public Health Officer in order to be accepted. We ended up talking for over two hours! We relayed all the programs that were signing up to be an Active Duty Officer. I remember my commissioning moment and how proud I was of myself. I still look back and smile. I knew I had chosen not just a job, but a profession.

My first day of officer's training began 4 September 2001. Our first week of training was more like in-processing, finding our Flights, and learning the basic command structure. We did daily PT as well. We were on our way out to PT the morning of September 11th, when we looked into one of the offices and saw what looked like a plane being flown into a building. Our cadre ushered us pretty quickly outside to start PT. Within minutes we were back inside the building while the cadre was preparing to give us the shock of our lives. Our training did not follow a normal pattern after that. There were many things we were not allowed to do because of the current security level. We did spend a lot of quiet time watching CNN and trying to figure out what happened. There were shocked faces and lots of looks of concern- it is one thing to join the military in a time of peace, but what happens when a significant event like 9/11 occurs? No one expects things like that to happen. Our remaining days in training went pretty quickly. The training class behind us lost over 50% of its students. I guess no one really wanted to join the military with the smell of conflict in the air.

Officers have quite a different kind of military indoctrination- particularly medical officers. We go through someone known as Commissioned Officers Training (COT). We are already commissioned officers prior to training. Our training was supposed to help familiarize us with the Air Force medical command and terminology. We learned how to put our BDU's and

Blues- which for some was quite a harrowing experience. Learning how to blouse your pants over your boots for the first time can be a little traumatic. But the most significant experience that happened while I was in training, not only changed my life, but the lives of millions, upon millions of people. (Reflection of 9/11)

I am an Active Duty Officer. My current deployment was only seven months long so I am going back to Beale Air Force Base. Beale is about one hour from Sacramento and about two hours from San Francisco. It is a beautiful area- close to the coast and close to the mountains. The real next adventure will be what happens with the military next. Where do we go from here?

I remember the first time my sister came to visit me. I had to been on Active Duty for about six months. She saw me in my BDU's for the first time and she said it looked like I was playing dress up in our dad's old clothes! I guess I will always be the little sister. The first time I saw my parents, it didn't seem like things were any different. I still get taken care of and coddled when I am home. They are excellent parents!

I have been deployed twice. One for a couple of months in the Balkans and once for many months in Iraq. The Balkans deployment was wonderful. I inspected restaurants and other food establishments, as well as a slaughterhouse. I had a great time.

Iraq was an interesting experience. Everything has its good and bad moments. But every experience is what you make of it. I will remember this deployment for a lifetime. I was part of an Army Civil Affairs unit. Our job was to help rebuild the country. That definitely is not an easy task with mortars and rockets going off all around you and people being murdered every day. But you stay positive and remember who you are trying to help. We created a project to help empower Iraqi women. This by far is probably the best experience I have had in the military. We made something from scratch and delivered it to the local women- they said going to the course we created was the first time they had felt important in their life. We gave them an opportunity for education and advancement. That day that the women graduated from our course was an amazing day-we made a difference. You try and tune out the horrible things going on in the country and only hope that you have made some kind of difference. I can't change a country, but I certainly made an impact on seventeen wonderful Iraqi women.

About my homecoming, I am still here! But I expect to be in low key. I just want to get a ride from the airport to my house, drop off all my gear, take a shower without shower shoes, and sleep in my own bed. That isn't too much to ask.

War In The Camps (Jm's Story) Saddam Captured

In July 1997, I swore in and became an Army soldier for my country. I knew what direction I was looking for in my life, so the decision was an easy one. I wanted to leave my home and become my own man.

I am from a small family, my mom and dad always expected more of me because I am the oldest son. My younger brother got away with everything. We always went places with my grandparents. We always went on great family vacations. Currently I have one daughter, and my wife, who I met while stationed in Germany.

We have a new love for bulldogs and she is an expert on them now.

Boot camp was playing with ammunition and gunfire. Also we had to get up early in the morning and stay in shape. I was doing what I liked to do. I was training to fight for my country. We had obstacle courses; I learned pretty quickly who was in charge.

I graduated from boot camp to the next level and was stationed in Friedberg, Germany for seven and a half years. While I was there I received Infantry training and became interested in weapons training. I received details weapons training. This would prepare me for what I would be facing in the future.

I went to school to become a sniper. I had special qualifications to become a sniper. Being a sniper is a rough job. There are a lot of lonely nights, being positioned where you are needed. Sniper training involves learning to kill the enemy M-24, open rifle range training.

While being stationed to Iraq I encountered a sand storm. You cannot see, visibility is altered, and you cannot see your hand in front of your face. So you don't know where your enemy might be. I worked sixteen hour days; I was trained in Special Forces over watch.

The media is on the massive man hunt for the capture of evil tyrant, Saddam, he has been eluding Special Forces and the military. He seems to stay one step ahead of the manhunt, and continues to keep Iraqi's guessing his every move.

In December 2003 in Baghdad we are briefed about his location and Operation Red Dawn is now underway. It is very early in the morning we are positioned and move in to apprehend this evil man. He is in a foxhole in Tikrit, as we move in to surround him; he is dirty and unkempt, unshaven and surrendered right away. He is quickly put into zip cuffs and taken into Camp Victory in Baghdad. This is a day of victory for the history of Iraq. There are shouts of joy as he is taken to face the war crimes he has committed.

In April 2003 while in Baghdad I am shot in the left leg while in enemy fire. I have been trained to finish my missions; I jumped off the building and continue my missions for the next four hours. I am then taken to get medical attention. It takes a while to heal. I have been awarded a purple heart for bravery. I also have been awarded The Army Combination Medal. "I am very proud to serve our country. "

I can best describe coming back home to my home in the states as unbelief. You are so excited to hear from your loved ones, spend quality time without the fear of enemy fire, memories haunt you, and in the lives you have taken and have had to protect your family unit. The family you cherish has had to be put on hold.

Good experiences while being away was our platoon trained Iraqi soldiers; we helped to deliver school supplies to the children, their smiles you never forget. Played soccer with Iraqi people, and gave sport equipment to the children. My fondest memory was meeting President Bush at Christmas in Baghdad. We shook hands with the man who had our future in his hands.

Bad experiences come with a war torn country that has been trying to survive the mortal combat and enemy zone, being where you are not wanted. Seeing death on a daily basis. The facets of death from severely wounded to putting dog tags on the fallen heroes and victims of circumstance. I have driven through three roadside bombings and I am still here. Senseless killing of innocent victims who just happen to be in the wrong place at the wrong time. Suicide bombers who don't care or "devalue" human life.

I am due to be deployed in July 2007. I will defend my country and the American way of life as I set out to the battle zone, and try not to think about my life back at home until I return to my homeland. While I am here I will not miss any opportunity to enjoy my life with my family. Every waking moment I am not over there I will excel over here.

Blue Horizons (Ah's Story) On American Soil

I committed to the Navy in 1997; in September of 1998 I went to boot camp. Still not sure why I joined, but so far it seems to be the right decision. Boot camp was much less an eye opener. The first week, we were very deprived of sleep. All they wanted to do was to break everybody down mentally in order to rebuild us as a" team." I will say that it did work very well. The part that still sticks out the most in my mind is when I was less than a week from graduation day; I had been really sick and had finally decided to go to medical. Well, when I was walking back to my berthing, I went the wrong way down the sidewalk and was stopped by a Chief. He proceeded to give me a "ticket." I never told my division P.O. because I was afraid of being held back. Well I was never caught and did graduate on time.

The best part was when we had graduated our form of "hell week." They stood us in formation and had the entire division take of their recruit ball caps and gave us a Navy ball cap. It's considered the point of cross over from boot camp to the real Navy. I don't think a single one of us had dry eyes; it was the feeling of relief, happiness, and being proud of our accomplishments.

The first time I went home was after boot camp, it was filled with good times with family and friends. The trip home that I remember the most is after a ten month deployment in the Gulf. My family decided to have a big get together as a welcome home for myself and a goodbye for my cousin. It was such a great day to see all the family and friends. It was a beautiful summer day, a little warm, but very low humidity. My cousin had just completed her officer training and all of the relatives wanted to see the two of us salute each other (she was an officer). Well, they never got their wish, I love my cousin dearly and have the utmost respect for her but she had only been in the grind for about a year and I was at five years already. I told everyone that when she wasn't so wet behind the ears that I would let them have her salute photo.

I haven't experienced a lot while on foreign land but the things that I have experienced will never be forgotten. I did see a country that is in shambles. For the most part, people wanted our help but with what they had been put through in the past, they were afraid to ask for it for fear of their lives. There were a lot of destroyed buildings, random ammunition shells just lying around like we would see leaves on the ground in the fall. Many families separated, whether they were missing or deceased. Very unorganized i.e. No leadership.

I have visited about a dozen other countries now while en route to the gulf and each one has its interesting things to see and do, and the not so interesting. ** There are stories to tell but I'd rather not tell them at this time.

When I returned from my first deployment, I was only twenty years old and had been married about a year. My oldest son was three weeks old to the day when we returned. My mom and dad had drove out from MN and picked up my wife, Lynda and our son. Then they drove down to San Diego to meet the ship when it pulled pier side. I was allowed to be third person off of the ship because of being a new father. When I was walking down the brow I almost tripped. I happened to look up and the amount of people just amazed me and I about froze.

My next trip home, I was really worried that my son wouldn't recognize me. When I left he was about two and a half, but when I returned, he was three and a half. I was in charge of making sure all of the semis were loaded quick and proper, so all the personnel and commands would have their gear in a few days. I came down with my coveralls on and immediately saw my family, so I walked over to the fence and my son reached through and grabbed my hat right off my head. It was such a relief that he still recognized me by sight. I think the only reason that he did is because this is what he saw me go to work in everyday, and on the weekends he would try to wear my boots and put on the hat.

After that I was up for new orders, shore duty, finally, so Lynda and I decided to stay out here in Lemoore. We had another little boy about a year later. I think the toughest job for a family being in the military is the spouse that stays home. All I have to do is pack my bags and say goodbye and go to work as always, just in a different environment. My wife, Lynda has to continue to work forty hours a week and still take care of the boys. At the same time being able to explain why daddy isn't home, taking care of the bills, and all the other day to day things that go on.

Home Sweet Home (Sp's Story)

I joined the Air Force in June of 1996. I joined the Air Force to serve my country, to learn a new trade and to travel the world.

I am married and have two daughters. Both my girls are the light of my life. Each is unique and wonderful. My wife is a great mother to my children. Children bring out the best in all of us. Our girls are poppy's and mom mom's girls.

Boot camp is being thrown together with sixty other guys from all different parts of the country, with their own way of doing things, but somehow learning to work as a team. Learning how to follow direct orders "NOW." Not having direct contact with my family and friends was hard. When allowed to call home, conversations had to be short and to the point. At one point my wife, who was then my girlfriend, was hospitalized. I had to wait for permission to call home to see if she was okay.

Another dramatic experience was the death of my best friend in an automobile accident. It was difficult to receive the news over the phone and not be able to reach out to the people I needed the most, or to be able to attend his services.

My next base was Sheppard Air Force Base, Texas. I spent the next eight months there learning the basics of Aircraft Mechanic. After leaving Sheppard Air Force Base, I moved to Little Rock Air Force Base to finish my formal training.

My first trip home was long awaited, since it was the longest amount of time I had ever been away from my family. So many changes happen when time flies and you are many miles away.

Some of the places I have deployed to are: South America, Antarctica, Canada, Germany, England, and the Middle East. I certainly got to travel and see parts of the world, I might not have otherwise seen.

Most of my experiences have been good; I have seen a lot of the world and have worked with some good people. The only bad experience I have had is seeing wounded soldiers being transported out of combat zones. One of my greatest experiences was being there to stand by the American flag at the South Pole.

The best part about coming home is getting to wrap your arms around your wife and kids. There is nothing better than seeing your kids standing there in a crowd of people waving the American flag, knowing they are proud of you.

Welcome Home (A Soldier's Saga) (Sh's Story)

I joined the Army National Guard in August of 1999. I joined a Multi-Role Bridge company in Mobridge, South Dakota and went to Basic Training in February of 2000. I went to my advanced individual training (AIT) immediately following and was trained in five ton dump trucks, 915 and 916 tractor trailers and primarily the twenty ton crane.

I joined the military for the tuition assistance at college as well as for the GI Bill to assist with school payments. I decided to contract in the ROTC program in order to receive a commission into the army. I volunteered for Active duty because I knew that I could always go back to South Dakota to establish myself, however if I stayed in the state from the start it would have been a lot harder to leave later in life to go see the world. And see the world I have!

I was born and raised on a small farm in a rural community in Southwest, MN growing up as an only child, I spent a lot of time playing outside, creating things, and helping dad at any chance I could get. I am truly a "tomboy" so I love the outdoors. My hobbies include riding horse, roller blading, crocheting, scrap booking, and spending time with family and friends. My father is self employed electrical contractor and my mother is a homemaker and cleans houses on the side.

Three experiences while at Basic Training include but are not limited to while at Basic Training (Boot camp) graduation I received an award for high marksmanship in the battalion, I qualified expert hitting thirty seven out of forty targets exposed. This was a huge accomplishment for me because prior to our final qualification I was having extreme difficulty, it turns out my weapon had a lose screw and my sight picture would change every time I fired. I kept my focus and kept trying, I had my weapon checked out by an armor and they tightened the screw and the next time I went on the firing line I fired a 37! I was overjoyed that day!

While at Basic Training I was in a leadership position for all nine weeks, I was squad leader for five weeks, and then the Platoon guide for four weeks, this really motivated me to work hard and to stay focused to remain the leadership positions.

Additionally at Basic Training I received an Award for Soldier Leader of the Cycle, this was voted on by my peers as well as my drill sergeants for the rotation, and this meant that I looked up upon my peers as well as the drill sergeants as a leader.

When I graduated from Basic Training I went home to South Dakota and drilled once a month and went back to College of South Dakota State University (SDSU). I continued to drill in the SD National Guard and also joined the ROTC program at SDSU, I graduated in May of 2002 with a Bachelor Science degree in Animal Husbandry and I also received my commission into the Engineer Corps in the United States Army.

My first duty station (and only duty station) while on active duty was Fort Hood, Texas. I arrived in August 2003 and volunteered for my first deployment in December 2003. I left for Iraq the first time on my birthday March 2004. I was the Executive Officer for a Topographic Engineer Company. It was then I received the Support Platoon Leader position. This platoon consisted of topographic surveyors as well as radio operators. The surveyors were tasked with completing boundary surveys of the base camps which US soldiers were housed at.

I was deployed from March 2004- December 2004 and again from December 2005-December 2006. I was stationed in Baghdad, Iraq for both deployments.

My first trip home from Iraq was in December 2004. I did not tell my parents the real dates which I would be coming home and so they thought I was going to miss Christmas. I showed up on their door step on the 23rd December at noon, I rang the doorbell and nobody bothered to get up to answer the door, (they thought it was my uncle). Once I opened the door I thought I was going to give them both a heart attack, they were in shock but extremely happy to have me home. What! a homecoming. My parents were hosting the family Christmas that year, and so we kept it a secret from the rest of the family and surprised everyone as they arrived for Christmas, what a Christmas present that was.

My experiences were different for both deployments; the first time around we were mortared every couple of nights, and so it got to point where I could hardly sleep at night because I was afraid to go to sleep until the mortars hit and then I knew I would be safe for the rest of the night. They mortared us on what seemed like clock work. When I got back home to the US, I would jump when I would hear loud startling noises. Things still bother me today when I am not expecting a noise or paying attention.

The second deployment we were mortared maybe four times the entire year, so a lack of sleep was not due to nerves this time around. This time it was because of the long hours spent at the office. My second deployment I worked as a Battalion Adjutant so my days were filled with preparing and overseeing of awards, evaluations, social functions, legal actions, promotions, finance actions, and award and promotion ceremonies.

This last employment I arrived back in the United States in early December 2006. My parents were in the gym when my unit walked in and was welcomed home. They were able to spend a few days with me in Texas and then I was able to go home about a week later to spend Christmas at home again. It was a hard transition home this time around. I was so used to working fourteen to sixteen hour days, that I was not used to having so much unstructured time. Something that people do not understand is that life stood still for the years I spent in Iraq. It is like that time does not exist. So when family or friends have gotten married or have had children, you miss out on all those little things and when you get home, they expect you to fit right in. (you feel like an outsider looking in). But you do not; it is kind of like you are a stranger in your own family or around your friends until you are reacquainted with things. Losing precious memories of time, the sands through the hour glass, these are the days of your life. Time swiftly brings changes and throws us curve balls in this life. Hold onto all the beautiful memories, "snap shots of your life."

I will be leaving Active duty in May of 2007 (ETSing). I am very excited to move back to South Dakota to be near my friends and family once again. I thank the Lord for all the blessings and opportunities which I have experienced through the military, as well as for all the great friends I have met in the service. I would also like to thank my parents for their dedicated support through thoughts, prayers and mail throughout my military service, without them my hardships would have been more difficult. "I am much honored to have served my country."

Tributary to A Soldier's Prayer

I wrote A Soldier's Prayer through the guidance of the Holy Spirit. I prayed continually for the heroes that needed a hedge of protection around them as they entered into their war zone destinations. I have had three nephews in the service; one has returned safely home the other two are still active. As you see through media outlets the faces of the fallen you realize that could be your child. Many of my friends and acquaintances are facing the same dilemma. Many of our comrades have fought in this war, just as in times past. While they continue to fight for our freedom we as a nation need to continually have them in our thoughts and prayers. God is our shield and protector, we can call on Him in times of trouble and He will hear our plea. He is our rescuer; we must humble ourselves as a nation unto His authority. We need to stay One Nation Under God.

A Soldier's Prayer

Lord watch over us as we are far away, let the light of your spirit visit us today. May we praise you; worship you, as we walk day by day. Protect us in the heat of the night

*dear lord we pray, surround us with your love as a father
protects his child, comfort us and keep us close to thy side.
Watch over our children, our families and our loved ones
to, we know dear Lord to trust only you.*

Dedicated to all the serviceman and women who serve us for the freedom of our nation. May the light of the savior shine in your lives. Amen. Tina M. Ray 4-20-05

This poem is also dedicated to Support our Troops/ Tiny Hands for the ministry of helping our troops get the much needed supplies sent to them in love. May God continue to bless the hands of Support our Troops/ Tiny Hands.

Tributary To
The Battle Cry Is At The Door

When you are reading scripture in Gods word and something sticks out at you, you can become inspired to write what God wants you to write, this has happened to me in the very early hours of the morning, I am trying to sleep but my mind is wandering and the words are filling my soul to overflowing and when I get up, and get journaling. God's word reveals to me what I am to write. The Battle Cry is at the Door was one of these poems that was so inspirationally presented that I said wow! The poem talks about war and rumors of war.

The Battle Cry Is At The Door

There is a day coming, when darkness shall come, It is the day of the Lord, the battle's begun. Can't you hear the battle cry, it is at the door. There will be rumors, rumors of war. We must put on our armor and help others in need; they need to see our lights shine for the cause indeed. For perilous times shall come, there will be famine in our land. Come Christian soldier, it is time to take a stand. Stand for Jesus, for He's the mighty king, and when you hear the victor's cry, you to will sing. "The Battle Cry is at the Door, let truth march on we must endure".

I have chosen to dedicate this poem to my big brother (one of eight) Gary Lee; who has always looked out for his little sister, and has been my protector as I was growing up. Thank you, Gary. Gary has an only son who is serving in the military and has been on a tour of duty to Afghanistan and is expecting his first child in early summer. Congratulations! And may God bless your family.

Research Acknowledgements

Books Read: Seventh Addition American Presidents by David C. Whitney

American History by Brian Lamb

The Unfinished Nation by Alan Brinkley

American Facts and Dates by Gorton-Carruth

The Declaration of Independence by Stephanie Schwartz Driver

Web Pages Read: www.ushistory.org/declaration/document

www.archives.gov/national-archives-experience/charters

www.ustreas.gov/education/fact-sheets/history

www.rfcnet.org/news

www.aetheists.org/courthouse

www.sullivan-county.com/news/mine/case
noprayer.htm

www.infoplease.com

www.aish.com/jewishissues/middleeast

www.antiwar.com/casualties/

www.hinduonnet.com

www.globalpolicy.org/intljustice

www.cnn.com/amishshooting/2006

News and Articles Read: CNN NEWS, FOX NEWS,
TIME MAGAZINE

Author's Notes

I would like to take the time to thank each and every person who purchases my book, to be able to support our men and women who are fighting for our freedom as we speak. They're dedication and hard work is so honorable. They give up their families and friends to fight for our country. The times that they are away we move on with our lives, but do we really realize the huge sacrifice they are making in our world? I would like to continue to lift them up in prayer to our almighty God, who will bring us through this trial. Thank you to the soldiers who gave their time to interview for my book. That was such a blessing! Recognizing and honoring what you do for our great country stirs my joyful soul.

When we are against all odds, and things look the darkest, remember the light of the world, Jesus, who shone His love light through onto Calvary onto a sin cursed world and gave His only son that we as sinners could become redeemed by the blood of the lamb. He gave us the gift of eternal life. Exalt His Holy Name.

Prayerfully,
Tina M.Ray

CROSSING ENEMY LINES ONE NATION UNDER GOD

Is The Third Book By Author Tina M. Ray

This book is my first novel and offers months of research of how the birth of a nation was brought forth, how our founding fathers shaped the great nation of United States of America through the laws and constitutions brought to our land and people through the power of prayer, it also represents prayer out of our school systems and the ramifications of what has happened since this was done. The war saga of war times we are facing and have been since the war began. The land history of our allies. Israel's role in the Middle East its allies and Gods' time table of events. "The time of Jacob's trouble" as predicted in the bible. The four horsemen who will bring sorrow in the times of tribulation. The stories of soldiers who are in the battle zone for our freedom. The war as seen through a soldier's eyes. The descriptive nature of the reality of war and its casualties. The terrorist cell groups who have been programmed through their evil leader and his demise. The battle between good verses evil, in which good always wins. Prophetical prophecy of world futuristic events that are to take place at a point in history. The King of Kings and Lord of Lords to rule and reign from His father's throne in the Mount of Olives in the holy land. A percentage of sales from this book will be for the ministry of getting phone cards for the military. AT&T phone cards, "Let Freedom Ring" will be a small part of giving back to the servicemen and women who are in the heat of the battle for my freedom. May God bless you as you read the words He has inspired upon my heart through this novel, and may you continue to pray for the situation in the Middle East, but rest assured God is in control and through His awesome power and might He will bring us through. Praise! His wonderful mercy and grace.

About the Author

Tina lives with her husband, Gary in Cecil County. They attend Restoration Family Worship Center in Peach Bottom, Pennsylvania. Wendle Pell is the pastor. Wendle is also the lead singer in his group Blue Grass and Truth. Tina and Gary are very active in their church and with church socials. They're love for bluegrass gospel shines in their lives. Tina has developed a love for mandolin and is learning how to play. Gary is learning banjo. Together they are learning songs to give praise to their king Jesus. I thank God every day for my church family, members of the group and their families, and our love of music, fellowship, and brotherhood. Praise God! May The Lord put a song in your hearts and a tap to your toes as you go by the path He has led you to today, just remember it was Jesus, who paved the road to righteousness and has put a light unto your path leading you unto Himself. Give Him the glory!